With Best Wishes
To my Dear Friends

The Hollombes

Helen
Rubenstein

July 1968

EMMA LAZARUS

EMMA LAZARUS

(July 22, 1849 — November 19, 1887)

Selections from Her Poetry and Prose

Edited, with an Introduction, by
MORRIS U. SCHAPPES

Third Revised and Enlarged Edition

EMMA LAZARUS FEDERATION
OF JEWISH WOMEN'S CLUBS
150 Fifth Avenue, New York, N. Y. 10011

1967

MORRIS U. SCHAPPES has long been regarded as a distinguished American Jewish historian, literary critic and teacher. Since 1958 he has been the Editor of *Jewish Currents*.

His published works include *The Jews in the United States: A Pictorial History (1654-1954); A Documentary History of the Jews in the United States, 1654-1875; The Letters of Emma Lazarus, 1868-1885.*

He has also contributed articles and reviews to the *American Jewish Historical Society Publications, Minnesota History, Publications of the Modern Language Association, American Literature, The Saturday Review, Jewish Life, New Masses, Mainstream, Chicago Jewish Forum, Jewish Social Studies,* and other periodicals.

First Edition, 1944
Copyright by IWO Jewish-American Section
Second Printing, 1945
Revised and Enlarged Edition, 1947
Third Revised and Enlarged Edition, September 1967
Copyright © 1967 by
MORRIS U. SCHAPPES
Library of Congress Catalog Card Number: 67–30299

PRINTED IN THE U.S.A.
412

TABLE OF CONTENTS

TRANSLATIONS

PROSE

IN TRIBUTE TO CLARA LICHT, 1889-1964

Clara was born in the city of Rovno, Russia, March 14, 1889 and raised in the Pale of Jewish settlement in the Ukraine, under the rule of the Tsar, where opportunities were extremely limited.

The family was poor. Clara's father was a scholar, a linguist and grammarian. This student of the Talmud, in which the sages had inscribed labor and learning as the highest commandments for the human race, inspired his sons and daughters to earn their bread as workers and to help build a just world.

Clara's mother, my mother-in-law by marriage to her daughter Libbie, was a sunny personality and similar to Beruriah of Babylon and Glückel of Hamelin (Germany). Like many of the women in her immediate vicinity, she spread her protecting wings over the family in a spiritual aura bespeaking tolerance, courage and hope. Even in her old age, in our home in Brooklyn, she read the best volumes of our private Yiddish library.

In a basement cold and damp, on the edge of a river in the town of Rovno, six children were raised, among them Clara.

With the tacit approval of the parents, who were fearful but proud of their children's courageous deeds, the home was the center of the underground movement against the Tsarist evil regime. At the age of 14-15 Clara was entrusted with serious assignments by the leading committee and, looking younger than her age, was able to elude the police. When finally the secret agents were on her track, Clara had to leave the country. She came to America after the unsuccessful Russian Revolution in 1905.

Like her proletarian brothers and sisters, Clara worked in the sweat shops in Philadelphia and in New York. Her husband, Noah Licht, was an ironworker, a union man active in cultural and fraternal organizations. It was only natural that Clara, renewing her activities in this country, should continue with a steady vigor and determination defying all obstacles.

Clara was now the product of two different socio-economic and cultural systems; born in autocratic Russia and transplanted to democratic America, where the roots of Thomas Jefferson were strong and the valiant spirit of Eugene V. Debs was expressed in action by the American working masses. The growth of American democracy was not the exclusive prerogative of men. Women of great intellect, courage and high spirit were relentless in their battles for equal rights for women, for the abolition of slavery and for trade union organization. Famous among them were Susan B. Anthony and Erenstine L. Rose. Mother Jones's activities in the trade union field (she was Clara's contemporary) imbued the latter with determination, as did the poetry of social protest by Sarah Cleghorn.

A daughter of a persecuted but vigorous people, Clara Licht derived from Jewish history and culture additional strength to perceive and fight for democracy and justice. And Clara fought! She never studied the biblical sources nor ancient history, but in her typical, indomitable way she paraphrased the eloquent words of Deborah of ancient days, urging the masses to unite for the welfare of the people.

Clara rarely recited from Emma Lazarus' writings, but she ably and intelligently translated the ideals of that great woman-author into actual organizational achievements at literally thousands of gatherings in which she participated or helped organize. Emma Lazarus' maxim that the home of the Jews is wherever they find freedom was clearly translated by Clara's maintaining that there is, there will be liberty, where Jews alongside others fight to extend and perpetuate it. Clara's greatest strength was her steadfastness in the battles for principles and convictions.

Clara's conception of the woman's role in society was clear and unequivocal. The contribution of American women to the growth of American democracy was an axiom. The outstanding role of Jewish women in the land was as it remains, beyond question. It was due to this general understanding of the problem that Clara considered her activities among the Jewish women of utmost importance, especially among the working women.

Thus Clara was one of the co-founders and builders of the Emma Lazarus Federation of Jewish Women's Clubs, making her special contribution by organizing many clubs in Brooklyn. From its inception to the last days of her consciousness, Clara devoted to the Emma Lazarus Federation and clubs every ounce of her vigor and responsibility.

Her loyalty to the organization was due to its broad principles of humanism as expressed in the writings of I. L. Peretz, Sholem Aleichem, the Yiddish poets and in the prose and poetry of Emma Lazarus.

Clara was not only known to many people; she knew hundreds of men and women in various communities, many by their first names. She rarely knew the addresses of her friends, acquaintances and co-workers, but she could lead you to the streets and the buildings in which they lived.

Clara was a housewife and a mother of two married sons. We, the family, highly valued the indomitable spirit of that Gibraltar-like woman. Her grandchildren knew her not as their "sitter" during babyhood; Clara had no time for it. They loved "gramma" for her devotion to humanity; they appreciated the depth and breadth of her philosophy.

Clara was a great idealist. In her philosophical concepts she envisioned a society based on equality shared by all. In that sense she worked for posterity. But Clara participated in the activities of her community pragmatically, elastically and patiently for the daily mundane needs sought and craved by all human beings in our society.

When the annals of the sixty years of this turbulent century will be written and read, Clara's name will be there as a shining example of conscious devotion to the great cause of humanity, freedom, peace and justice.

BEN FIELD

INTRODUCTION

There is only one reason why people should read the work of Emma Lazarus today, but that is reason enough: she can still delight, stir, inspire, and instruct.

Her sonnet, "The New Colossus," placed in 1903 on a plaque affixed to the Statue of Liberty, is known to millions, many of whom however do not even know that she wrote it. Of those who do, too few know that she wrote anything else. Yet that sonnet comes out of a profound and intense experience that was itself only one part and one expression of something broader and richer.

For many years now her writings have been practically inaccessible to the general public. The two volumes of her poetry, collected and published posthumously in 1889, have long been out of print and are virtually out of the market. Her prose is buried away in the brittle, yellow pages of magazines of the 1880's.

This little selection, which having compiled I now contemplate with chagrin because of all the valuable material I have been compelled to omit, is a beginning not only toward the rehabilitation of a needlessly dusty reputation. It is also, I believe, a contribution to the present intellectual and emotional life both of American Jews and of non-Jews here and abroad. Some day, and I hope it is soon, there may be a complete collection of her poetry and prose, including her letters, published in a more sumptuous edition, but it is in the spirit of Emma Lazarus herself that the present selection is issued in this form, now, without more delay. When, in 1882, she was urging *The American Hebrew* to publish her *Songs of a Semite*, she wrote to the magazine: "It is my idea to have the pamphlet issued at as low a price and in as simple a form as possible." Eager then for a popular audience, she saw to it that the paper-covered edition sold for twenty-five cents. Only two or three years before that she had, with unflattering objectivity, written to Edmund Clarence Stedman, the literary critic and editor, lamenting that she had "accomplished nothing to stir, nothing to awaken, to teach or to suggest, nothing that the world could not equally well do without." But by 1882, having been so deeply stirred herself, she was awakening others; and she was driven to seek as wide an audience as possible. Our judgment today must be "that the world could not equally well do without" the work of Emma Lazarus.

Born in New York on July 22, 1849, Emma Lazarus was brought up in the wealthy and fashionable home of her father, Moses, who was in the sugar refining industry until his retirement in 1865 at the age of fifty-two. Her great-grandparents (Samuel Lazarus on her father's side and Simon Nathan on her mother's) had been in this country at the time of the American Revolution.

Shy and sensitive, she always clung closely to a family circle that was knit in intimacy with unusual tightness. Emma's education was wholly with private tutors, who apparently encouraged her to master foreign languages that were to extend her horizons. Thus when, in her seventeenth year, her first collection is published under the title, *Poems and Translations,* it includes translations from Hugo, Dumas, Schiller, and Heine. In 1871, when *Admetus and Other Poems* appears, she reveals a command of Italian in her translation of Leopardi, continues to translate Heine, and adds Goethe to her list. Later she was to translate from Petrarch and Alfred de Musset; and in the last years of her tragically short life she studied Hebrew in order to be able to translate from the Hebrew poets of medieval Spain without the intermediary of the German versions of these poets that she had formerly used.

From the beginning, also, some of her interests were topical, to the extent at least that the Civil War and its aftermath penetrated to her comparatively sheltered existence and stimulated her to poetic compositions of unexpected dignity in one so young. Nevertheless, even after her second book had been issued and favorably received both in England and here, Thomas Wentworth Higginson, abolitionist distinguished especially for his command of a Negro regiment in the Civil war and also an outstanding man of letters, wrote to his sisters from Newport in 1872, after making Emma's acquaintance: ". . . She is rather an interesting person, . . . she has never seen an author till lately, though she has corresponded with Emerson. It is curious to see how mentally famished a person may be in the very best society."

It was not to be many years before authors and other men of affairs were to be speaking of her in different terms. That she was handsome, her picture demonstrates. But she was to prove intelligent far beyond the expectations even of men gallant and liberal enough to concede that women might have brains. To a growing circle she was to show that, in certain circumstances, the tepid grace of "femininity" could combine with intellectual strength to produce a character both ardent and firm. But I am anticipating my account . . .

If fashionable society could not adequately nourish an Emma Lazarus, books did, and, in Emerson's view, somewhat too exclusively. Emerson, already in his mid-sixties, was not too old to recognize a fresh and youthful talent in her first volume in 1866, especially when he found such a note of earnestness in it. Corresponding with her particularly in 1868 and 1869, he encouraged her and helped directly to shape her mind. He suggested she read Marcus Antoninus, the *Bhagvat Geeta*, and Thoreau and Walt Whitman, but most of all Shakespeare for economy and effectiveness of rhetoric. She had sent him "Admetus," which he hailed as "a noble poem," an opinion in which he was not shaken even when William Dean Howells, the country's outstanding novelist and editor, rejected it for publication in *The Atlantic Monthly*.

Emerson guided her to a process of condensation that improved the work. Yet he acutely put his finger on a major problem in the development of Emma Lazarus when he wrote to her on January 20, 1869: ". . . I do not know but the sole advice I have to offer is a pounding on the old string, namely, that though you can throw yourself so heartily into the old world of Memory, the high success must ever be to penetrate into & show the celestial element in the despised Present, & detect the deity that still challenges you under all the gross and vulgar masks." In her maturity Emma Lazarus was to write movingly of the Present, but she was to grow in such a way that even when she wrote of Yesterday it was because that particular Past was timely and a signpost to Tomorrow.

In 1876, when she visited for a wonderful week with Emerson at his home, she left for him the proof-sheets of *The Spagnoletto*, a five act verse tragedy with the scene laid in Italy in 1655. Emma insisted on publishing it only, however, for "private circulation." Three or four years later she composed the powerful drama, *The Dance to Death*, a story of the persecution of the Jews in Thuringia (Germany) in 1349. For several years she kept it unpublished; but when events in Europe proclaimed the utter timeliness of it, she published it serially in *The American Hebrew* from June 30 to September 1, 1882, and then made it the main work in her proudly titled pamphlet, *Songs of a Semite*.

17

The two subjects, her treatment of them, and her own attitude to them are landmarks in the growth of Emma Lazarus.

After the cordial reception accorded *Admetus and Other Poems* in 1871, she turned her hand to a prose romance based on an incident in Goethe's life, published in 1874 as *Alide*. She sent a copy to Turgenev, then in France, whose novel about Russian nihilists, *Virgin Soil*, had so much impressed her, and received in reply a very warm commendation, dated September 2, 1874: ". . . I am truly glad to say that I have read your book with the liveliest interest: It is very sincere and very poetical at the same time; the life and spirit of Germany have no secret for you—and your characters are drawn with a pencil as delicate as it is strong. I feel very proud of the approbation you give to my works—and of the influence you kindly attribute to them on your own talent; an author, who writes as you do—is not a 'pupil in art' any more; he is not far from being himself a master." Even generous words from such a source, however, did not lead Emma Lazarus to continue to write narrative prose. In fact she published little prose until 1881, when her biographical sketch of Heine appeared as an introduction to her volume of translations of his poems. When she used prose again, it was chiefly the prose of controversy and exhortation, a prose used in the defense of her people.

Most of those who have written about Emma Lazarus, both in her own time and more recently, have fallen prey to a confusing exaggeration. To dramatize a point that has its own sufficient drama, they have resorted to melodrama. They would have us believe that until the Russian pogroms of the 1880's she had no interest in Jews or the problems of Jews, that she had virtually no consciousness of being a Jew. Evidence to the contrary is neglected or explained away.

The source of this needlessly strained interpretation is probably the biographical sketch included in the edition of her poems published in 1889, a sketch written by her own sister, Josephine. Therein we are told, for instance, that in 1881, when Emma Lazarus wrote the essay on Heine for her volume of translations, "she is as yet unaware or only vaguely conscious of the real bond between them," the fact that they were both Jewish. The reader is invited to judge for himself from the excerpts given within. Again, the fact that in *The Century* of April 1882 there appeared her article, "Was the Earl of Beaconsfield [Disraeli] a Representative Jew?" is taken to signify that even then Judaism was "a dead letter to her. . . . Nor had she any great enthusiasm for her own people." We are informed that "by a curious, almost fateful juxtaposition" the same issue of *The Century* carried an anti-Semitic defense of the Russian pogroms, and that it was in reaction to this article, to which Emma Lazarus replied most vigorously, that she suddenly found herself to be Jewish.

Now it is true that the events in Russia and Madame Z. Ragozin's apology for them evoked a qualitative change in Emma Lazarus' consciousness of and activity in behalf of the Jews. But it will help us understand and appreciate the full significance of this change if we do not ignore the existing elements without which that change could not have taken place.

The record as I read it, however, shows that a Jewish consciousness was present in Emma Lazarus from her earliest days as a young writer.* There is her poem, written at the age of eighteen, "In the Jewish Synagogue at Newport," published in her volume, *Admetus and Other Poems,* and immediately reprinted in *The Jewish Messenger.* There is her life-long interest in Heine, whose position as a Jew she so thoroughly understood and so brilliantly analyzed. There are her translations from Gabirol and Halevy, published in *The Jewish Messenger* early in 1879. There is the aid she gave Dr. Gustav Gottheil of Temple Emanu-El "for some years before 1882" in his work on a collection of hymns and anthems adapted for Jewish worship. And, perhaps most significant, there is the fact that she wrote her profoundly moving play, *The Dance to Death,* a "few years" before it was published in 1882.

Then what was the character of the transformation that Emma Lazarus underwent? It was not from no interest in Jewry or a lack of interest to a sudden espousal of the cause of the Jew. Consciousness and interest there had always been, but it was an interest in Jewry distant and past, not present and American. The nature of the American Jewish community, however, must be remembered. In 1848, the year before her birth, there were only about 50,000 Jews in the entire country (out of a total population of about 23,000,000). By 1880, the number of Jews had increased to over 300,000, with the population as a whole having grown to more than 50,-000,000. The social composition of this American Jewry had become largely middle-class; the majority were native-born.

---

* See the Appendix for a detailed discussion of the evidence for this conclusion.

There was an absence of those Jewish working class *masses* that we knew recently and that did not in fact begin to come into our country in great numbers until the very pogroms of the 1880's drove them out of Russia and East-Central Europe.

In such a context, her interest in Jewry was extensive but placid. She felt herself confronted with no *problems* that she and other Jews had to solve. No action was required. The persecuted Jews of fourteenth century Germany, whose condition and courage she dramatizes in *The Dance to Death*, were long dead, and conditions in Germany had been changed. In general the extension of democracy was easing the burden of the Jew. Her sympathies were all with the oppressed, whose history she was reading, but it was a passive sympathy because she saw no present issue.

Such an issue was presented, to the world and to Emma Lazarus, by the Russian pogroms that began in 1879 and increased in extent and ferocity during the next years. The pogroms evoked a passionate reaction she had not known before, and led her into active struggle against the brutalities abroad that her imagination rendered so vivid and her conscience made so personal. Now there was work to be done, refugees to be cared for, American Jews to be aroused to participation in the defense of a kin they were slow to recognize, too slow at least to suit Emma Lazarus. To enrich and to make more effective this new activity of hers, literary and otherwise, she found it necessary to enlarge and intensify her studies in Jewish history. Such was the new pattern of her life, fashioned out of old elements, but fired in the furnace of zealous activity.

Having access, because of her previous work, to non-Jewish magazines of distinction, she carried the intellectual struggle into these organs, publishing some of her most stirring prose and poetry in periodicals like *The Century* and *The Critic*. But while she battled the anti-Semitic enemy with one hand in these publications, she was using the other to arouse American Jewry itself to her own heightened sense of responsibility and fraternity. *The American Hebrew* grew in stature as she became for several years a regular contributor of drama, poetry, and prose. She developed a passion for Jewish history, but not for theology. Her concern was not so much with the articles of Jewish faith as with the plight of the Jewish people. She rewrote in prose and sang in poetry the vital lessons that could solve the problems of the Jews of the 1880's. The heroes, scholars and poets of the Jewish people—Bar Kochba and Raschi, Gabirol and Halevy —she made more than ever her own, and shared them with her people.

To Jew and non-Jew she presented with eloquence her concept of, and findings about, the Jews. The Jews loved life and nature. The Jews were thinkers whose thoughts had influenced both the Christian and Mohammedan world. The Jews were tough-fibered and resistant; oppression could bend but not break them, scatter them but not destroy. Jews were an able and resourceful people; they tended to excel in whatever pursuits were open to them.

The Jews needed and loved freedom. She wrote: "Until we are all free, we are none of us free." She wrote again: "Today, wherever we are free, we are at home." Jews sought learning first, and wealth only secondarily, and that generally when they felt wealth was their only protection against insult. Their banner bore the democratic word Justice rather than the condescending or sentimental word Charity. Jews were rebels, not dogmatists. "The Jew (I say it proudly rather than deprecatingly) is a born rebel. He is endowed with a shrewd, logical mind, in order that he may examine and protest; with a stout and fervent heart, in order that the instinct of liberty may grow into a consuming passion, whereby, if need be, all other impelling motives shall be swallowed up." Jews would follow the truth, therefore, wherever it lead, despite the fact that for the Jew it so often led to persecution. Maybe others—non-Jews—also shared these ideals. But the non-Jews were the *dominant* Christians and could have applied their principles—yet so often did not—and oh so often hounded the Jews for trying to do so. These things she learned and these she taught in words noble and stark.

To whom did she speak them? She looked about her. American Jewry seemed to her comfortable, self-centered, indifferent too often to the condition of Jews in undemocratic countries in Europe. What did they have in common, they thought, with the thin-faced, pale, Ghetto-Jew, earlocks long, "the caftaned wretches" of East Europe? In words without malice but sharp and stinging she told the rich American Jew that his freedom depended on the state of the pogrom-ridden Jews of the Caucasus. The American Jews may have squirmed, but

21

they heeded her, when she issued the challenge: where is the
American Ezra who will lift the Banner of the Jew and use it
as an international battle-standard? Perhaps some of them
even reflected that the American Ezra might be named Emma.

She visited the Jewish immigrants arriving from Russia and
huddled in the refuges on Ward's Island. She studied them
and their plight, these Jews who had, by law and terror, been
kept out of so many of the productive pursuits of mankind.
With Heine she noted that each country gets the Jews it deserves or the Jews that it makes (a theme that recurs: see
"Raschi in Prague" and "Russian Christianity versus Modern
Judaism"). What Jews would our country make, and get? In
the United States the Jew was "the free citizen of a Republic."
Several times she noted the fateful fact that 1492 was the year
in which the Jews were driven from Spain while Columbus
was discovering America to "bequeath a Continent to Freedom." (See "1492" and "By the Waters of Babylon.") The
more conscious of her Jewishness Emma Lazarus became, the
prouder she grew of America. She wrote: "We possess the
double cosmopolitanism of the American and the Jew."

It is true she observed and felt the existence of anti-Semitism
in the land. When an anti-Semitic article appeared in *The Sun,*
the New York daily, she complained in a letter to Philip Cowen
"that this contempt and hatred underlies the general tone of
the community towards us, and yet when I even remotely hint
at the fact that we are not a favorite people I am accused of
stirring up strife and setting barriers between the two sects. . . ."
She even knew a Jew who was alarmed whenever another Jew
distinguished himself in any way because of the envy and antagonism such ability might arouse. But she would not be
hushed.

For her America was to be free, its democracy to be thoroughly tested. American Jews, these new immigrants especially,
must do everything—not only those few things allowed them
in European despotisms—they must farm and work and build
and trade and learn and create and teach. How she thrilled
when her friend Michael Heilprin showed her a letter from a
Russian immigrant settled in Texas, a farmer, happy, with
pogroms only a memory and with democratic sun overhead
(see "In Exile"). Manual training was needed. What Booker
T. Washintgon was to preach to the Negro people she taught
the Jews. They must conquer new forms of labor. Interest in
her idea spread. She lived to see the founding of The Hebrew

22

Technical Institute, of which she was acknowledged to be the original inspiration.

But how many Jews could come to this America? There must be other solutions. With democracy so limited in Europe —Czars, Kaisers, tyrants regnant so widely—Jews needed a home of their own, a state where they could become a nation again. George Eliot, to whom she dedicated *The Dance to Death,* had thought of it and had made her Daniel Deronda speak of it. Another English writer, Laurence Oliphant, traveling in Palestine, had repeated it. Emma Lazarus made the idea her own and began to discuss it with her special vigor in *The American Hebrew.* Her solution was not intended for American Jews, who, she made it clear, would, could, and should stay here. But the Russian Jew, the Polish, Rumanian, Hungarian—the oppressed and the haunted millions of Europe—they needed it. It was her answer to the lack of democracy on the Continent. Herzl's concept, to become known as Zionism, was still unheard of when she expressed her aspiration for the conditions of a normal national life for the Jews.

Furthermore, Emma Lazarus looked where it was forbidden and daring to look. In the Mosaic Code she found the ethics and foundation of the idea then so fresh—Socialism. She disputed with surprised Christians their claim to having originated Socialist ideals. The basis was in the Mosaic Code, she insisted. And wasn't Marx, weren't other leaders of the Socialist movement, Jews? Proudly she claimed her own.

In England, there was a poet whom she had long admired, imitated, and emulated, William Morris. He was a Socialist, a Marxian. When she went to England in the spring of 1883, she made sure to seek him out, spending a day with him at his factory in Surrey, and wrote about it for *The Century* in July, 1886, after she had met him again on her second trip to England. Morris and Socialism were being misrepresented. In the article she set out to explain how good and sincere Morris was, how his poetry had led him to his politics, and what his politics were. "The passion for beauty," she wrote of Morris and perhaps of herself too, "which unless balanced by a sound and earnest intelligence is apt to degenerate into sickly and selfish aestheticism, inflames him with a burning desire to bring all classes of humanity under its benign influence." Moses, Marx, and William Morris—she claimed them all.

If many, Jew and non-Jew, did not follow her in such sweep and boldness of thought, she did not press the point. If the Jews in America wrote and acted with full consciousness of their brethren in other lands, and also resisted the manifestations of anti-Semitism even here, her avowed mission would be accomplished. In London she had been received " with great distinction" by prominent Jewish leaders, some of whom were converted to advocacy of her views on a Jewish national state. Non-Jews in literary and social circles had also honored her as poet and Jew. She returned refreshed and inspirited in the fall of 1883, taking again to her writing and public work. But within the year personal calamity overtook her. In August 1884 she became ill. On March 9, 1885 the father she loved so dearly died, and the blow was heavy. In May she went again to Europe, stayed more than two years, visited England, then The Hague, Paris, Pisa, Florence, Rome, while all the time the fatal cancer devastated her. She could not help comparing herself to Heine, similarly racked with illness and dying by degrees on his "mattress-grave." But despite the wasting horror of the body, the mind was alert and reaching out to new fields. To her devotion to music and the theater was now added a zest for serious study of painting; she left unfinished a work on the "genius and personality" of Rembrandt.

In December, 1883 she wrote, in the new form of the prose-poem, the last work she was to live to see published. "By the Waters of Babylon," printed in *The Century* in March 1887, is the beautiful summation of her character and ideals, and of her most mature style. In 1880, in the poem, "Echoes," Emma Lazarus had expressed the feeling that she was handicapped because she was a woman and alone. "Late-born and woman-souled," she was "one in love with solitude and song." She dared not "cope . . . with the world's strong-armed warriors." Not hers to "recite the dangers, wounds, and triumphs of the fight." She thought then she was one "who veiled and screened by womanhood must grope." But in the last five or six years of her life she strode from solitude into a fighting fraternity with her people that made her a leader of Jews on two continents and of the American people as a whole too. These words of Liebhaid von Orb's in *The Dance to Death* have a poignancy beyond that of the drama itself:

> *God help me! Shall my heart crack for love's loss*
> *That meekly bears my people's martyrdom?*
> *He lives—I feel it—to live or die with me.*
> *I love him as my soul—no more of that.*

I am all Israel's now—till this cloud pass,
I have no thought, no passion, no desire,
Save for my people.

Having imaginatively written these words a few years before 1882, she lived them fully after that year.

When she returned from Europe to New York on July 31, 1887 she was grievously ill. She died on November 19, 1887, and was buried in the family lot at Beth El Fields, Cypress Hills, N.Y.

Emma Lazarus was widely mourned. She was more than a literary figure. From London, Robert Browning cabled to *The American Hebrew* that he "associates himself with the admiration for the genius and love of the character of his lamented friend . . ." John G. Whittier, the venerable warrior and poet, wrote: "Since Miriam sang of deliverance and triumph by the Red Sea, the Semitic race has had no braver singer. 'The Crowing of the Red Cock,' written when the Russian sky was red with blazing Hebrew homes, is an indignant and forceful lyric worthy of the Maccabean age. Her 'Banner of the Jew,' has the ring of Israel's war trumpets." The Southern writer, George W. Cable, expressed perhaps the conscience she had stimulated among non-Jews when he declared: ". . . she was the worthy daughter of a race to which the Christian world owes a larger debt of gratitude, incurred from the days of Abraham until now, and from which it should ask more forgiveness than to and from any other people that ever trod the earth."

There were many similiar statements in the Memorial Number of *The American Hebrew*, December 9, 1887 and in a later issue, October 5, 1888: from Claude G. Montefiore in London, from Edmund C. Stedman, from Edward Eggleston, preacher, historian, and Hoosier Schoolmaster, from Professor Hjalmar H. Boyesen of Columbia University, from John Hay, novelist, biographer of Lincoln, and Secretary of State, from E. L. Godkin of the *Post* and Dana of the *Sun*, from Harriet Beecher Stowe and Thomas Wentworth Higginson, from poets, critics, and leaders of the Jewish community.

In her youth, Emerson had directed her to the reading of Walt Whitman, the great poet of our democracy. After her death, Whitman said to Horace Traubel one day: "She must have had a great, sweet, unusual nature."

Her name and her sonnet are fittingly wrought in metal on the pedestal of the Statue of Liberty. When America needed a poet to express what America meant to the world and to

Americans, it turned to Emma Lazarus. As more Americans, Jewish and non-Jewish, come to know more of her work, she will resume a place in their hearts and minds that still needs to be filled. She led us briefly while she lived, and her thoughts led us for a time after she died. But there is more in Emma Lazarus than is remembered. We need that more.

MORRIS U. SCHAPPES

PREFACE TO REVISED AND ENLARGED EDITION

The cordial reception accorded the first edition, and the continual demand for the work of Emma Lazarus since the second edition went out of print, has encouraged the publishers to issue the work again. I have therefore taken the opportunity to add two items: the poem "The New Ezekiel" and a hitherto unpublished letter to Henry George that I discovered among the Henry George Papers in the Manuscript Division of the New York Public Library, through the courtesy of which I am permitted to include it. In the Introduction I have made minor revisions on pages 16 and 17.

M. U. S.

New York, September 26, 1947

PREFACE TO THE NEW EDITION

In the 23 years that have passed since this little collection was first issued, the reputation of Emma Lazarus has grown both in literary and general circles.

In 1949, for the centennial of her birth, the New York Public Library published my collection, *The Letters of Emma Lazarus, 1868-1885.* University dissertations on her work have been written by, among others, Arthur Zeiger and Aaron Kramer. Two biographies have been published. The first, in 1949, *The World of Emma Lazarus* by H. E. Jacob, was factually irresponsible (see my reviews in *Masses and Mainstream,* July, 1949 and in *American Literature,* January, 1950). Much more reliable and illuminating was *Emma Lazarus, Woman with a Torch,* 1956, by Eve Merriam, herself a poet. This book, like the present reprint, was sponsored by the Emma Lazarus Federation of Jewish Women's Clubs. In 1959, Eve Merriam reworked her book for teenagers, under the title, *The Voice of Liberty, The Story of Emma Lazarus.*

What is still needed is an ample selection of her poetry, prose and letters. Until such a volume is published, I am pleased to have the opportunity to present a new edition of the original selections in order to keep her own writings, even in this modest form, before the growing public aware of the significance, in poetry and in American Jewish life and literature, of the work of Emma Lazarus.

In the Introduction, I have made corrections and revisions on pages 14, 15, 16, 17, 18, 19, 20, 21, 22, 23 and 24, and *passim* in the notes in the text.

M. U. S.

New York, June 24, 1967

Poems

AUGUST MOON

. . .

"I am one
Who would not restore that Past,
Beauty will immortal last,
Though the beautiful must die—
This the ages verify.

. . .

I behold, without regret,
Beauty in new forms recast,
Truth emerging from the vast,
Bright and orbed, like yonder sphere,
Making the obscure air clear.
He shall be of bards the king,
Who, in worthy verse, shall sing
All the conquests of the hour,
Stealing no fictitious power
From the classic types outworn,
But his rhythmic line adorn
With the marvels of the real.
He the baseless feud shall heal
That estrangeth wide apart
Science from her sister Art.

. . .

ECHOES

Late-born and woman-souled I dare not hope,
The freshness of the elder lays, the might
Of manly, modern passion shall alight
Upon my Muse's lips, nor may I cope
(Who veiled and screened by womanhood must grope)
With the world's strong-armed warriors and recite
The dangers, wounds, and triumphs of the fight;
Twanging the full-stringed lyre through all its scope.
But if thou ever in some lake-floored cave
O'erbrowed by rocks, a wild voice wooed and heard,

Answering at once from heaven and earth and wave,
Lending elf-music to thy harshest word,
Misprize thou not these echoes that belong
To one in love with solitude and song.

VENUS OF THE LOUVRE

Down the long hall she glistens like a star,
The foam-born mother of Love, transfixed to stone,
Yet none the less immortal, breathing on.
Time's brutal hand hath maimed but could not mar.
When first the enthralled enchantress from afar
Dazzled mine eyes, I saw not her alone,
Serenely poised on her world-worshipped throne,
As when she guided once her dove-drawn car,—
But at her feet a pale, death-stricken Jew,
Her life adorer, sobbed farewell to love.
Here *Heine* wept! Here still he weeps anew,
Nor ever shall his shadow lift or move,
While mourns one ardent heart, one poet-brain,
For vanished Hellas and Hebraic pain.

THE CHOICE

I saw in dream the spirits unbegot,
Veiled, floating phantoms, lost in twilight space;
For one the hour had struck, he paused; the place
Rang with an awful Voice:
                    "Soul, choose thy lot!
Two paths are offered; that, in velvet-flower,
Slopes easily to every earthly prize.
Follow the multitude and bind thine eyes,
Thou and thy sons' sons shall have peace with power.
This narrow track skirts the abysmal verge,
Here shalt thou stumble, totter, weep and bleed,
All men shall hate and hound thee and thy seed,
Thy portion be the wound, the stripe, the scourge.
But in thy hand I place my lamp for light,

Thy blood shall be the witness of my Law,
Choose now for all the ages!"
                                    Then I saw
The unveiled spirit, grown divinely bright,
Choose the grim path. He turned, I knew full well
The pale, great martyr-forehead shadowy-curled,
The glowing eyes that had renounced the world,
Disgraced, despised, immortal Israel.

IN THE JEWISH SYNAGOGUE AT NEWPORT

Here, where the noises of the busy town,
    The ocean's plunge and roar can enter not,
We stand and gaze around with tearful awe,
    And muse upon the consecrated spot.

No signs of life are here: the very prayers
    Inscribed around are in a language dead;
The light of the "perpetual lamp" is spent
    That an undying radiance was to shed.

What prayers were in this temple offered up,
    Wrung from sad hearts that knew no joy on earth,
By these lone exiles of a thousand years,
    From the fair sunrise land that gave them birth!

Now as we gaze, in this new world of light,
    Upon this relic of the days of old,
The present vanishes, and tropic bloom
    And Eastern towns and temples we behold.

Again we see the patriarch with his flocks,
    The purple seas, the hot blue sky o'erhead,
The slaves of Egypt,—omens, mysteries,—
    Dark fleeing hosts by flaming angels led.

A wondrous light upon a sky-kissed mount,
    A man who reads Jehovah's written law,
'Midst blinding glory and effulgence rare,

Unto a people prone with reverent awe.

The pride of luxury's barbaric pomp,
   In the rich court of royal Solomon—
Alas! we wake: one scene alone remains,—
   The exiles by the streams of Babylon.

Our softened voices send us back again
   But mournful echoes through the empty hall;
Our footsteps have a strange, unnatural sound,
   And with unwonted gentleness they fall.

The weary ones, the sad, the suffering,
   All found their comfort in the holy place,
And children's gladness and men's gratitude
   Took voice and mingled in the chant of praise.

The funeral and the marriage, now, alas!
   We know not which is sadder to recall;
For youth and happiness have followed age,
   And green grass lieth gently over all.

And still* the sacred shrine is holy yet,
   With its lone floors where reverent feet once trod.
Take off your shoes as by the burning bush,
   Before the mystery of death and God.
                                        July 27, 1867.

THE DAY OF DEAD SOLDIERS*
May 30, 1869

Welcome, thou gray and fragrant Sabbath-day,
   To deathless love and valor dedicate!
Glorious with the richest flowers of May,
   With early roses, lingering lilacs late,
With vivid green of grass and leaf and spray,

---

* Emma Lazarus herself on September 13, 1887 changed the word
"Nathless" to "And still."

33

Thou bringest memories that far outweigh
　　The season's joy with thoughts of death and fate.
　　　　　•　　　•　　　•

Who knows what tremulous, dusky hands set free,
　　Deck quaintly with gay flowers the graves unknown?
What wealth of bloom is shed exuberantly,
　　On the far grave in Illinois alone,
Where the last hero, sleeping peacefully,
Beyond detraction and mistrust, doth lie,
　　By the glad winds of prairies overblown?

With hymns and prayer be this day sanctified,
　　And consecrate to heroes' memories;
Not with wild, violent grief for those who died,
　　O wives and mothers, but with patience wise,
Calm resignation, and a thankful pride,
That they have left their land a fame so wide,
　　So rich a page of thrilling histories.

GIFTS

"O World-God, give me Wealth!" the Egyptian cried.
His prayer was granted. High as heaven, behold
Palace and Pyramid; the brimming tide
Of lavish Nile washed all his land with gold.
Armies of slaves toiled ant-wise at his feet,
World-circling traffic roared through mart and street,
His priests were gods, his spice-balmed kings enshrined,
Set death at naught in rock-ribbed charnels deep.
Seek Pharaoh's race to-day and ye shall find
Rust and the moth, silence and dusty sleep.

"O World-God, give me Beauty!" cried the Greek.
His prayer was granted. All the earth became
Plastic and vocal to his sense; each peak,

---

* Memorial Day had been established in 1868 by Major-General John A.
Logan in a General Order issued from the Headquarters of the Grand
Army of the Republic. May 30, 1869 fell on a Sunday.

34

Each grove, each stream, quick with Promethean flame,
Peopled the world with imaged grace and light.
The lyre was his, and his the breathing might
Of the immortal marble, his the play
Of diamond-pointed thought and golden tongue.
Go seek the sun-shine race, ye find to-day
A broken column and a lute unstrung.

"O World-God, give me Power!" the Roman cried.
His prayer was granted. The vast world was chained
A captive to the chariot of his pride.
The blood of myriad provinces was drained
To feed that fierce, insatiable red heart.
Invulnerably bulwarked every part
With serried legions and with close-meshed code,
Within, the burrowing worm had gnawed its home,
A roofless ruin stands where once abode
The imperial race of everlasting Rome.

"O Godhead, give me Truth!" the Hebrew cried.
His prayer was granted; he became the slave
Of the Idea, a pilgrim far and wide,
Cursed, hated, spurned, and scourged with none to save.
The Pharaohs knew him, and when Greece beheld,
His wisdom wore the hoary crown of Eld.
Beauty he hath forsworn, and wealth and power.
Seek him to-day, and find in every land.
No fire consumes him, neither floods devour;
Immortal through the lamp within his hand.

THE BANNER OF THE JEW

Wake, Israel, wake! Recall to-day
    The glorious Maccabean rage,
The sire heroic, hoary-gray,

    His five-fold lion-lineage:
The Wise, the Elect, the Help-of-God,

35

The Burst-of-Spring, the Avenging Rod.*

From Mizpeh's mountain-ridge** they saw
    Jerusalem's empty streets, her shrine
Laid waste where Greeks profaned the Law,
    With idol and with pagan sign.
Mourners in tattered black were there,
With ashes sprinkled on their hair.

Then from the stony peak there rang
    A blast to ope the graves: down poured
The Maccabean clan, who sang
    Their battle-anthem to the Lord.
Five heroes lead, and following, see,
Ten thousand rush to victory!

Oh for Jerusalem's trumpet now,
    To blow a blast of shattering power,
To wake the sleepers high and low,
    And rouse them to the urgent hour!
No hand for vengeance—but to save,
A million naked swords should wave.

O deem not dead that martial fire,
    Say not the mystic flame is spent!
With Moses' law and David's lyre,
    Your ancient strength remains unbent.
Let but an Ezra*** rise anew,
To lift the *Banner of the Jew!*

A rag, a mock at first—erelong,
    When men have bled and women wept,
To guard its precious folds from wrong,
    Even they who shrunk, even they who slept,

---
    * The sons of Mattathias—Jonathan, John, Eleazar, Simon (also called
the Jewel), and Judas, the Prince.
    ** The Mizpeh was a place of solemn assembly for the Jews of Palestine
at the time of the Maccabean revolt against Antiochus IV, 175-164 B.C.
    *** See Book of Ezra, Old Testament.

Shall leap to bless it, and to save.
Strike! for the brave revere the brave!*

THE NEW YEAR
Rosh-Hashanah, 5643 (1882)

Not while the snow-shroud round dead earth is rolled,
  And naked branches point to frozen skies,—
When orchards burn their lamps of fiery gold,
  The grape glows like a jewel, and the corn
A sea of beauty and abundance lies,
            Then the new year is born.

Look where the mother of the months uplifts
  In the green clearness of the unsunned West,
Her ivory horn of plenty, dropping gifts,
  Cool, harvest-feeding dews, fine-winnowed light;
Tired labor with fruition, joy and rest
            Profusely to requite.

Blow, Israel, the sacred cornet! Call
  Back to thy courts whatever faint heart throb
With thine ancestral blood, thy need craves all.
  The red, dark year is dead, the year just born
Leads on from anguish wrought by priest and mob,
            To what undreamed-of morn?

For never yet, since on the holy height,
  The Temple's marble walls of white and green
Carved like the sea-waves, fell, and the world's light
  Went out in darkness,—never was the year
Greater with portent and with promise seen,
            Than this eve now and here.

Even as the Prophet promised, so your tent

---

* This poem was first read at the closing exercises of the Temple
Emanu-El Religious School, New York, then appeared in *The Critic*,
June 3, 1882, and was reprinted in *The American Hebrew*, June 9, 1882.

Hath been enlarged unto earth's farthest rim.
To snow-capped Sierras from vast steppes ye went,
   Through fire and blood and tempest-tossing wave,
For freedom to proclaim and worship Him,
               Mighty to slay and save.

High above flood and fire ye held the scroll,
   Out of the depths ye published still the Word.
No bodily pang had power to swerve your soul:
Ye, in a cynic age of crumbling faiths,
Lived to bear witness to the living Lord,
               Or died a thousand deaths.

In two divided streams the exiles part,
   One rolling homeward to its ancient source,
One rushing sunward with fresh will, new heart.
   By each the truth is spread, the law unfurled,
Each separate soul contains the nation's force,
               And both embrace the world.

Kindle the silver candle's seven rays,
   Offer the first fruits of the clustered bowers,
The garnered spoil of bees. With prayer and praise
   Rejoice that once more tried, once more we prove
How strength of supreme suffering still is ours
               For Truth and Law and Love.

THE CROWING OF THE RED COCK

Across the Eastern sky has glowed
   The flicker of a blood-red dawn,
Once more the clarion cock has crowed,
   Once more the sword of Christ is drawn.
A million burning rooftrees light
The world-wide path of Israel's flight.

Where is the Hebrew's fatherland?
   The folk of Christ is sore bestead;
The Son of Man is bruised and banned,

Nor finds whereon to lay his head.
His cup is gall, his meat is tears,
His passion lasts a thousand years.

Each crime that wakes in man the beast,
  Is visited upon his kind.
The lust of mobs, the greed of priest,
  The tyranny of kings, combined
To root his seed from earth again,
His record is one cry of pain.

When the long roll of Christian guilt
  Against his sires and kin is known,
The flood of tears, the life-blood spilt,
  The agony of ages shown,
What oceans can the stain remove,
From Christian law and Christian love?

Nay, close the book; not now, not here,
  The hideous tale of sin narrate,
Reechoing in the martyr's ear,
  Even he might nurse revengeful hate,
Even he might turn in wrath sublime,
With blood for blood and crime for crime.

Coward? Not he, who faces death,
  Who singly against worlds has fought,
For what? A name he may not breathe,
  For liberty of prayer and thought.
The angry sword he will not whet,
His nobler task is—to forget.

IN EXILE

*"Since that day till now our life is one unbroken paradise.
We live a true brotherly life. Every evening after supper we
take a seat under the mighty oak and sing our songs."—Extract
from a letter of a Russian refugee in Texas.*

Twilight is here, soft breezes bow the grass,
    Day's sounds of various toil break slowly off,
The yoke-freed oxen low, the patient ass
    Dips his dry nostril in the cool, deep trough.
Up from the prairie the tanned herdsmen pass
    With frothy pails, guiding with voices rough
Their udder-lightened kine. Fresh smells of earth,
The rich, black furrows of the glebe send forth.

After the Southern day of heavy toil,
    How good to lie, with limbs relaxed, brows bare
To evening's fan, and watch the smoke-wreaths coil
    Up from one's pipe-stem through the rayless air.
So deem these unused tillers of the soil,
    Who stretched beneath the shadowing oak-tree, stare
Peacefully on the star-unfolding skies,
And name their life unbroken paradise.

The hounded stag that has escaped the pack,
    And pants at ease within a thick-leaved dell;
The unimprisoned bird that finds the track
    Through sun-bathed space, to where his fellows dwell;
The martyr, granted respite from the rack,
    The death-doomed victim pardoned from his cell,—
Such only know the joy these exiles gain,—
Life's sharpest rapture is surcease of pain.

Strange faces theirs, wherethrough the Orient sun

---

* The letter was shown to Emma Lazarus by Michael Heilprin (1823-
1888), who had come to this country in 1856. In 1879-1880 he published
the first two volumes of *Historical Poetry of the Ancient Hebrews*. He
was very active in aiding the refugees from the pogroms.

Gleams from the eyes and glows athwart the skin.
Grave lines of studious thought and purpose run
From curl-crowned forehead to dark-bearded chin.
And over all the seal is stamped thereon
Of anguish branded by a world of sin,
In fire and blood through ages on their name,
Their seal of glory and the Gentiles' shame.

Freedom to love the law that Moses brought,
To sing the songs of David, and to think
The thoughts Gabirol to Spinoza taught,
Freedom to dig the common earth, to drink
The universal air—for this they sought
Refuge o'er wave and continent, to link
Egypt with Texas in their mystic chain,
And truth's perpetual lamp forbid to wane.

Hark! through the quiet evening air, their song
Floats forth with wild sweet rhythm and glad refrain.
They sing the conquest of the spirit strong,
The soul that wrests the victory from pain;
The noble joys of manhood that belong
To comrades and to brothers. In their strain
Rustle of palms and Eastern streams one hears,
And the broad prairie melts in mist of tears.

THE FEAST OF LIGHTS (*Hanuka*)

Kindle the taper like the steadfast star
Ablaze on evening's forehead o'er the earth,
And add each night a lustre till afar
An eightfold splendor shine above thy hearth.
Clash, Israel, the cymbals, touch the lyre,
Blow the brass trumpet and the harsh-tongued horn;
Chant psalms of victory till the heart take fire,
The Maccabean spirit leap new-born.

Remember how from wintry dawn till night,

Such songs were sung in Zion, when again
On the high altar flamed the sacred light,
    And, purified from every Syrian stain,
The foam-white walls with golden shields were hung,
    With crowns and silken spoils, and at the shrine,
Stood, midst their conqueror-tribe, five chieftains sprung
    From one heroic stock, one seed divine.

Five branches grown from Mattathias' stem,
    The Blessed John, the Keen-Eyed Jonathan,
Simon, the fair, the Burst-of-Spring, the Gem,
    Eleazar, Help-of-God; o'er all his clan
Judas the Lion-Prince, the Avenging Rod,
    Towered in warrior-beauty, uncrowned king,
Armed with the breastplate and the sword of God,
    Whose praise is: "He received the perishing."

They who had camped within the mountain-pass,
    Couched on the rock, and tented neath the sky,
Who saw from Mizpah's heights the tangled grass
    Choke the wide Temple-courts, the altar lie
Disfigured and polluted—who had flung
    Their faces on the stones, and mourned aloud
And rent their garments, wailing with one tongue,
    Crushed as a wind-swept bed of reeds is bowed,

Even they by one voice fired, one heart of flame,
    Though broken reeds, had risen, and were men,
They rushed upon the spoiler and o'ercame,
    Each arm for freedom had the strength of ten.
Now is their mourning into dancing turned,
    Their sackcloth doffed for garments of delight,
Week-long the festive torches shall be burned,
    Music and revelry wed day with night.

Still ours the dance, the feast, the glorious Psalm,
    The mystic lights of emblem, and the Word.
Where is our Judas? Where our five-branched palm
    Where are the lion-warriors of the Lord?

Clash, Israel, the cymbals, touch the lyre,
  Sound the brass trumpet and the harsh-tongued horn,
Chant hymns of victory till the heart take fire,
  The Maccabean spirit leap new-born!

RASCHI IN PRAGUE*

• • •

Then Raschi, who had stood erect, nor quailed
From glances of hot hate or crazy wrath,
Now sank his eagle gaze, stooped his high head,
Veiling his glowing brow, returned the kiss
Of brother-love upon the Christian's hand,
And dropping on his knees, implored the three,
"Grace for my tribe! They are what ye have made.
If any be among them fawning, false,
Insatiable, revengeful, ignorant, mean—
And there are many such—ask your hearts
What virtues ye would yield for planted hate,
Ribald contempt, forced, menial servitude,
Slow centuries of vengeance for a crime
Ye never did commit? Mercy for these!
Who bear on back and breast the scathing brand
Of scarlet degradation, who are clothed
In ignominious livery, whose bowed necks
Are broken with the yoke. Change these to men!
That were a noble witchcraft simply wrought,
God's alchemy transforming clods to gold.
If there be one among them strong and wise,
Whose lips anoint breathe poetry and love,
Whose brain and heart served ever Christian need—

---

* Raschi (1040-1105), the great rabbinical scholar, was the first to write
a commentary on the Talmud and the Bible; the name is con-
tracted from the initials of Rabbi Solomon Izhaki. The following took
place before the scene excerpted here: Raschi of Troyes, having toured
through Spain, Italy, Greece, Palestine, Egypt, Persia, and the Caucasus,
comes to Prague and is ceremoniously received by the chief Rabbi, Jochanan
ben-Eleazar. Duke Vladislaw is incited by Narzerad, "half whose wealth
was pledged to the usurers," and by the Bishop of Olmutz to order the arrest of Raschi and Jochanan and to prevent the guards from protecting Jews
against mob attacks. The soldiers carry out the arrest, breaking in on a
noon-day meal, rob, beat, and insult the old Rabbi, and drag them both to
the Duke, who addresses Raschi contemptuously. . . .

And there are many such—for his dear sake,
Lest ye chance murder one of God's high priests,
Spare his thrice-wretched tribe! Believe me, sirs,
Who have seen various lands, searched various hearts,
I have yet to touch that undiscovered shore,
Have yet to fathom that impossible soul,
Where a true benefit's forgot; where one
Slight deed of common kindness sown yields not
As now, as here, abundant crop of love.
Every good act of man, our Talmud says,
Creates an angel, hovering by his side.
Oh! what a shining host, great Duke, shall guard
Thy consecrated throne, for all the lives
Thy mercy spares, for all the tears thy ruth
Stops at the source. Behold this poor old man,
Last of a line of princes, stricken in years,
As thy dead father would have been to-day.
Was that white beard a rag for obscene hands
To tear? a weed for lumpish clowns to pluck?
Was that benignant, venerable face
Fit target for their foul throats' voided rheum?
That wrinkled flesh made to be pulled and pricked,
Wounded by flinty pebbles and keen steel?
Behold the prostrate, patriarchal form,
Bruised, silent, chained. Duke, such is Israel!"
"Unbind these men!" commanded Vladislaw.
"Go forth and still the tumult of my town.
Let no Jew suffer violence. Raschi, rise!
Thou who hast served the Christ—with this priest's life,
Who is my spirit's counselor—Christ serves thee.
Return among thy people with my seal,
The talisman of safety. Let them know
The Duke's their friend. Go, publish the glad news!"
Raschi the Saviour, Raschi the Messiah,
Back to the Jewry carried peace and love.
But Narzerad fed his venomed heart with gall,
Vowing to give his fatal hatred vent,
Despite a world of weak fantastic Dukes
And heretic bishops. He fulfilled his vow.

AN EPISTLE

FROM JOSHUA IBN VIVES OF ALLORQUI TO HIS FORMER
MASTER, SOLOMON LEVI-PAUL, DE SANTA-MARIA, BISHOP OF
CARTAGENA, CHANCELLOR OF CASTILE, AND PRIVY
COUNCILOR TO KING HENRY III OF SPAIN*

[In this poem I have done little more than elaborate and
versify the account given in Graetz's *History of the Jews* (Vol.
VIII, page 77), of an Epistle actually written in the beginning
of the 15th century by Joshua ben Joseph Ibn Vives to Paulus
de Santa Maria.—E. L.]

VI.

For I, thy servant, gather in one sheaf
   The venomed shafts of slander, which thy word
Shall shrivel to small dust. If haply grief,
   Or momentary pain, I deal, my Lord,
Blame not thy servant's zeal, nor be thou deaf
   Unto my soul's blind cry for light. Accord—
Pitying my love, if too superb to care
For hate-soiled name—an answer to my prayer.

VII.

To me, who, vine to stone, clung close to thee,
   The very base of life appeared to quake
When first I knew thee fallen from us, to be
   A tower of strength among our foes, to make
'Twixt Jew and Jew deep-cloven enmity.

---

* Rabbi Solomon Levi of Burgos (c. 1351-1435) turned Christian in
1391, during a bloody massacre of the Jews. His wife and son renounced
him. He became an instrument of Pope Benedict XIII in his schismatic
rivalry with Cardinal Pedro, the Pope at Avignon. After that he held many
high offices, constantly attacking Jews and Judaism. Joshua ben Joseph Ibn
Vives was a physician and Arabic scholar in Lorca, and a former pupil of
the apostate. In sending the poem to *The American Hebrew*, where it was
published June 16, 1882, Emma Lazarus wrote: "It has a strong bearing
on the question of the day, besides having a curious historic interest."

I have wept gall and blood for thy dear sake.
But now with temperate soul I calmly search
Motive and cause that bound thee to the Church.

VIII.

Four motives possible therefore I reach—
   Ambition, doubt, fear, or mayhap—conviction.
I hear in turn ascribed thee all and each
   By ignorant folk who part not truth from fiction.
But I, whom even thyself didst stoop to teach,
   May poise the scales, weigh this with that confliction,
Yea, sift the hid grain motive from the dense,
Dusty, eye-binding chaff of consequence.

●   ●   ●

XIX.

For some (I write it with flushed cheek, bowed head),
   Given free choice 'twixt death and shame, chose shame,
Denied the God who visibly had led
   Their fathers, pillared in a cloud of flame,
Bathed in baptismal waters, ate the bread
   Which is their new Lord's body, took the name
Marranos the Accursed, whom equally
Jew, Moor, and Christian hate, despise, and flee.

●   ●   ●

XX.

Even one no less than an Abarbanel
   Prized miserable length of days, above
Integrity of soul. Midst such who fell,
   Far be it, however, from my duteous love,
Master, to reckon thee. Thine own lips tell
   How fear nor torture thy firm will could move.
How thou midst panic nowise disconcerted,
By Thomas of Aquinas wast converted!

XXI.

Truly I know no more convincing way
    To read so wise an author, than was thine.
When burning Synagogues changed night to day,
    And red swords underscored each word and line.
That was a light to read by! Who'd gainsay
    Authority so clearly stamped divine?
On this side, death and torture, flame and slaughter,
On that, a harmless wafer and clean water.

• • •

XXV.

Where are the signs fulfilled whereby all men
    Should know the Christ? Where is the wide-winged peace
Shielding the lamb within the lion's den?
    The freedom broadening with the wars that cease?
Do foes clasp hands in brotherhood again?
    Where is the promised garden of increase,
When like a rose the wilderness should bloom?
Earth is a battlefield and Spain a tomb.

• • •

XXXIV.

Help me, O thou who wast my boyhood's guide,
    I bend my exile-weary feet to thee,
Teach me the indivisible to divide,
    Show me how three are one and One is three!
How Christ to save all men was crucified,
    Yet I and mine are damned eternally.
Instruct me, Sage, why Virtue starves alone,
While falsehood step by step ascends the throne.

Thou two-faced year, Mother of Change and Fate,
Didst weep when Spain cast forth with flaming sword,
The children of the prophets of the Lord,
Prince, priest, and people, spurned by zealot hate.
Hounded from sea to sea, from state to state,
The West refused them, and the East abhorred.
No anchorage the known world could afford,
Close-locked was every port, barred every gate
Then smiling, thou unveil'dst, O two-faced year,
A virgin world where doors of sunset part,
Saying, "Ho, all who weary, enter here!
There falls each ancient barrier that the art
Of race or creed or rank devised, to rear
Grim bulwarked hatred between heart and heart!"

THE NEW COLOSSUS*

Not like the brazen giant of Greek fame,
With conquering limbs astride from land to land;
Here at our sea-washed, sunset gates shall stand
A mighty woman with a torch, whose flame
Is the imprisoned lightning, and her name
Mother of Exiles. From her beacon-hand
Glows world-wide welcome; her mild eyes command
The air-bridged harbor that twin cities frame.
"Keep, ancient lands, your storied pomp!" cries she
With silent lips. "Give me your tired, your poor,
Your huddled masses yearning to breathe free,
The wretched refuse of your teeming shore.
Send these, the homeless, tempest-tost to me,
I lift my lamp beside the golden door!"

---

* Written in aid of Bartholdi Pedestal Fund, November 1883 [now inscribed on a plaque on the Statue of Liberty.-M.U.S.]

BAR KOCHBA*

Weep, Israel! your tardy meed outpour
  Of grateful homage on his fallen head,
That never coronal of triumph wore,
  Untombed, dishonored, and unchapleted.
If Victory makes the hero, raw Success
  The stamp of virtue, unremembered
Be then the desperate strife, the storm and stress
  Of the last Warrior Jew. But if the man
Who dies for freedom, loving all things less,
  Against world-legions, mustering his poor clan;
The weak, the wronged, the miserable, to send
  Their death-cry's protest through the ages' span—
If such an one be worthy, ye shall lend
  Eternal thanks to him, eternal praise.
Nobler the conquered than the conqueror's end!

BY THE WATERS OF BABYLON**

Little Poems in Prose

NO. I. THE EXODUS (August 3, 1492)

1. The Spanish noon is a blaze of azure fire, and the dusty pilgrims crawl like an endless serpent along treeless plains and bleached high-roads, through rock-split ravines and castellated, cathedral-shadowed towns.

2. The hoary patriarch, wrinkled as an almond shell, bows painfully upon his staff. The beautiful young mother, ivory-pale, well-nigh swoons beneath her burden; in her large enfolding arms nestles her sleeping babe, round her knees flock her little ones with bruised and bleeding feet. "Mother, shall we soon be there?"

3. The youth with Christ-like countenance speaks comfort-

---

* See "The Last National Revolt of the Jews" for the story of Bar Kochba, p. 100.
  ** The last work to be published in her lifetime, first appearing in *The Century*, March 1887.

ably to father and brother, to maiden and wife. In his breast, his own heart is broken.

4. The halt, the blind, are amid the train. Sturdy packhorses laboriously drag the tented wagons wherein lie the sick athirst with fever.

5. The panting mules are urged forward with spur and goad; stuffed are the heavy saddle-bags with the wreckage of ruined homes.

6. Hark to the tinkling silver bells that adorn the tenderly-carried silken scrolls.

7. In the fierce noon-glare a lad bears a kindled lamp; behind its network of bronze the airs of heaven breathe not upon its faint purple star.

8. Noble and abject, learned and simple, illustrious and obscure, plod side by side, all brothers now, all merged in one routed army of misfortune.

9. Woe to the straggler who falls by the wayside! No friend shall close his eyes.

10. They leave behind the grape, the olive, and the fig; the vines they planted, the corn they sowed, the garden-cities of Andalusia and Aragon, Estremadura and La Mancha, of Granada and Castile; the altar, the hearth, and the grave of their fathers.

11. The townsman spits at their garments, the shepherd quits his flock, the peasant his plow, to pelt with curses and stones; the villager sets on their trail his yelping cur.

12. Oh the weary march, oh the uptorn roots of home, oh the blankness of the receding goal!

13. Listen to their lamentation: *They that ate dainty food are desolate in the streets; they that were reared in scarlet embrace dung-hills. They flee away and wander about. Men say among the nations, they shall no more sojourn there; our end is near, our days are full, our doom is come.*

14. Whither shall they turn? for the West hath cast them out, and the East refuseth to receive.

15. O bird of the air, whisper to the despairing exiles, that to-day, to-day, from the many-masted, gayly-bannered port of Palos, sails the world-unveiling Genoese, to unlock the golden gates of sunet and bequeath a Continent to Freedom!

NO. V. CURRENTS.

1. Vast oceanic movements, the flux and reflux of immeasurable tides oversweep our continent.

2. From the far Caucasian steppes, from the squalid Ghettos of Europe,

3. From Odessa and Bucharest, from Kief and Ekaterinoslav,*

4. Hark to the cry of the exiles of Babylon, the voice of Rachel mourning for her children, of Israel lamenting for Zion.

5. And lo, like a turbid stream, the long-pent flood bursts the dykes of oppression and rushes hitherward.

6. Unto her ample breast, the generous mother of nations welcomes them.

7. The herdsman of Canaan and the seed of Jerusalem's royal shepherd renew their youth amid the pastoral plains of Texas and the golden valleys of the Sierras.

NO. VI. THE PROPHET.

1. Moses Ben Maimon lifting his perpetual lamp over the path of the perplexed;

2. Hallevi, the honey-tongued poet, wakening amid the silent ruins of Zion the sleeping lyre of David;

3. Moses, the wise son of Mendel, who made the Ghetto illustrious;

4. Abarbanel, the counselor of kings; Alcharisi, the exquisite singer; Ibn Ezra, the perfect old man; Gabirol, the tragic seer;**

5. Heine, the enchanted magician, the heart-broken jester;

6. Yea, and the century-crowned patriarch whose bounty engirdles the globe;—

7. These need no wreath and no trumpet; like perennial as-

---

* These cities were the sites of some of the pogroms that started in Russia in 1879 and spread to other countries nearby.

** Moses Maimonides (1135-1204), great Rabbi and scholar, author of *Mishnah;* Isaac ben Jehuda Abarbanel (1437-1508), minister of state of Alfonso V of Portugal and then chancellor to Ferdinand the Catholic, King of Castile, until driven into exile; Moses Mendelssohn (1729-1786), first great champion of Jewish emancipation in the 18th century, called the Luther of German Jewry for translating parts of the Bible into German; Judah B. Solomon B. Hophni Alcharisi, early 13th century Hebrew poet living in Spain; Moses Ben Jacob Ha-Sallah Ibn Ezra (c. 1070-c. 1138), Hebrew poet, linguist, and philosopher, living in Spain.

phodel blossoms, their fame, their glory resounds like the brazen-
throated cornet.

8. But thou—hast thou faith in the fortune of Israel? Wouldst
thou lighten the anguish of Jacob?

9. Then shalt thou take the hand of yonder caftaned wretch
with flowing curls and gold-pierced ears;

10. Who crawls blinking forth from the loathsome recesses of
the Jewry;

11. Nerveless his fingers, puny his frame; haunted by the bat-
like phantoms of superstition is his brain.

12. Thou shalt say to the bigot, "My Brother," and to the
creature of darkness, "My Friend."

13. And thy heart shall spend itself in fountains of love upon
the ignorant, the coarse, and the abject.

14. Then in the obscurity thou shalt hear a rush of wings,
thine eyes shall be bitten with pungent smoke.

15. And close against thy quivering lips shall be pressed the
live coal wherewith the Seraphim brand the Prophets.*

THE NEW EZEKIEL

What, can these dead bones live, whose sap is dried
    By twenty scorching centuries of wrong?
Is this the House of Israel, whose pride
    Is as a tale that's told, an ancient song?
Are these ignoble relics all that live
    Of psalmist, priest, and prophet? Can the breath
Of very heaven bid these bones revive.
    Open the graves and clothe the ribs of death?

Yea, Prophecy, the Lord hath said. Again
    Say to the wind, Come forth and breathe afresh,
Even that they may live upon these slain,
    And bone to bone shall leap, and flesh to flesh.
The Spirit is not dead, proclaim the word,
    Where lay dead bones, a host of armed men stand!
I ope your graves, my people, saith the Lord,
    And I shall place you living in your land.

---

* See *Isaiah*, VI, 5-6.

THE DANCE TO DEATH

A Historical Tragedy in Five Acts

This play is dedicated, in profound veneration and respect, to the memory of George Eliot, the illustrious writer, who did most among the artists of our day towards elevating and ennobling the spirit of Jewish nationality.

The scene: Partly in Nordhausen, partly in Eisenach. Time: May 4th, 5th, 6th, 1349.

(*Editor's Note*: In the first three acts, Rabbi Cresselin comes from Chinon, France, to the Free City of Nordhausen, to inform the Jews there that everywhere Jews are being persecuted and that in Nordhausen too they will all be burned. When Süsskind von Orb, the richest merchant in Thuringia, tells the congregation that they have nowhere to flee except to the Black Plague all around the city or to persecution elsewhere, Rabbi Cresselin repeats his warning, and dies. Schnetzen, enemy of Süsskind, incites Frederick, the Landgrave of Thuringia, against the Jews, blaming them for the Black Plague, and gets Frederick to instruct the Council of Nordhausen to burn them all, "Jews, Jewesses, and Jewlings." Frederick's son, Prince William, who is in love with Liebhaid von Orb and wants to marry her, intervenes for the Jews but is imprisoned by his father. Liebhaid is really Schnetzen's Christian daughter, whom Süsskind had rescued as an infant from the flames in which her mother died. Süsskind expects to save her life at least by revealing her identity, although Liebhaid later refuses and dies with them, saying to Süsskind, "Thy people are my people." The Nordhausen Council, having decided, with one dissenting vote, to carry out Frederick's order, has Süsskind and Rabbi Jacob brought before it to inform them of their doom.—M.U.S.)

ACT IV, SCENE 1

Enter SUSSKIND VON ORB *and* RABBI JACOB.

TETTENBORN.   Rabbi Jacob,
And thou, Süsskind von Orb, bow down, and learn
The Council's pleasure. You the least despised
By true believers, and most reverenced
By your own tribe, we grace with our free leave

To enter, yea to lift your voices here,
Amid these wise and honorable men,
If ye find aught to plead, that mitigates
The just severity of your doom. Our prince,
Frederick the Grave, Patron of Nordhausen,
Ordains that all the Jews within his lands,
For the foul crime of poisoning the wells,
Bringing the Black Death upon Christendom,
Shall be consumed with flame.

    RABBI JACOB (*springing forward and clasping his hands.*)
                          I' the name of God,
Your God and ours, have mercy!

    SUSSKIND.   Noble lords,
Burghers, and artisans of Nordhausen,
Wise, honorable, just, God-fearing men,
Shall ye condemn or ever ye have heard?
Sure, one at least owns here the close, kind name
Of Brother—unto him I turn. At least
Some sit among you who have wedded wives,
Bear the dear title and the precious charge
Of Husband—unto these I speak. Some here
Are crowned, it may be, with the sacred name
Of Father—unto these I pray. All, all
Are sons—all have been children, all have known
The love of parents—unto these I cry:
Have mercy on us, we are innocent,
Who are brothers, husbands, fathers, sons as ye!
Look you, we have dwelt among you many years,
Led thrifty, peaceable, well-ordered lives.
Who can attest, who prove we ever wrought
Or ever did devise the smallest harm,
Far less this fiendish crime against the State?
Rather let those arise who owe the Jews
Some debt of unpaid kindness, profuse alms,
The Hebrew leech's serviceable skill,
Who know our patience under injury,
And ye would see, if all stood bravely forth,
A motley host, led by the Landgrave's self,
Recruited from all ranks, and in the rear,

The humblest, veriest wretch in Nordhausen.
We know the Black Death is a scourge of God.
Is not our flesh as capable of pain,
Our blood as quick envenomed as your own?
Has the Destroying Angel passed the posts
Of Jewish doors—to visit Christian homes?
We all are slaves of one tremendous Hour.
We drink the waters which our enemies say
We spoil with poison,—we must breathe, as ye,
The universal air,—we droop, faint, sicken,
From the same causes to the selfsame end.
Ye are not strangers to me, though ye wear
Grim masks to-day—lords, knights and citizens,
Few do I see whose hand has pressed not mine,
In cordial greeting. Dietrich von Tettenborn,
If at my death my wealth be confiscate
Unto the State, bethink you, lest she prove
A harsher creditor than I have been.
Stout Meister Rolapp, may you never again
Languish so nigh to death that Simon's art
Be needed to restore your lusty limbs.
Good Hugo Schultz—ah! be those blessed tears
Remembered unto you in Paradise!
Look there, my lords, one of your council weeps,
If you be men, why, then an angel sits
On yonder bench. You have good cause to weep,
You who are Christians, and disgraced in that
Whereof you made your boast. I have no tears.
A fiery wrath has scorched their source, a voice
Shrills through my brain—"Not upon us, on them
Fall everlasting woe, if this thing be!"

    SCHNETZEN. My lords of Nordhausen, shall ye be stunned
With sounding words? Behold the serpent's skin,
Sleek-shining, clear as sunlight; yet his tooth
Holds deadly poison. Even as the Jews
Did nail the Lord of heaven on the Cross,
So will they murder all his followers,
When once they have the might. Beware, beware!

    SUSSKIND. So *you* are the accuser, my lord Schnetzen?

Now I confess, before you I am guilty.
You are in all this presence, the one man
Whom any Jew hath wronged—and I that Jew.
Oh, my offense is grievous; punish me
With the utmost rigor of the law, for theft
And violence, whom ye deemed an honest man,
But leave my tribe unharmed! I yield my hands
Unto your chains, my body to your fires;
Let one life serve for all.

    SCHNETZEN.   You hear, my lords,
How the prevaricating villain shrinks
From the absolute truth, yet dares not front his Maker
With the full damnable lie hot on his lips.
Not thou alone, my private foe, shalt die,
But all thy race. Thee had my vengeance reached,
Without appeal to Prince or citizen.
Silence! my heart is cuirassed as my breast.

    RABBI JACOB. Bear with us, gracious lords! My friend is
                          stunned.
He is an honest man. Even I, as 't were,
Am stupified by this surprising news.
Yet, let me think—it seems it is not new,
This is an ancient, well-remembered pain.
What, brother, came not one who prophesied
This should betide exactly as it doth?
That was a shrewd old man! Your pardon, lords,
I think you know not just what you would do.
You say the Jews shall burn—shall burn you say;
Why, good my lords, the Jews are not a flock
Of gallows-birds, they are a colony
Of kindly, virtuous folk. Come home with me;
I'll show you happy hearths, glad roofs, pure lives.
Why, some of them are little, quick-eyed boys,
Some, pretty, ungrown maidens—children's children
Of those who called me to the pastorate.
And some are beautiful tall girls, some, youths
Of marvellous promise, some are old and sick,
    Amongst them there be mothers, infants, brides,
Just like your Christian people, for all the world.

Know ye what burning is? Hath one of you
Scorched ever his soft flesh, or singed his beard,
His hair, his eyebrows—felt the keen, fierce nip
Of the pungent flame—and raises not his voice
To stop this holocaust? God! 't is too horrible!
Wake me, my friends, from this terrific dream.

•   •   •

TETTENBORN.   No more, no more!
Go, bid your tribe make ready for their death
At sunset.
    RABBI JACOB.   Oh!
    SÜSKIND.   At set of sun today?
Why, if you travelled to the nighest town,
Summoned to stand before a mortal Prince,
You would need longer grace to put in order
Household effects, to bid farewell to friends,
And make yourself right worthy. But our way
Is long, our journey difficult, our judge
Of awful majesty. Must we set forth,
Haste-flushed and unprepared? One brief day more,
And all my wealth is yours!
    TETTENBORN.   We have heard enough.
Begone, and bear our message.
    SUSSKIND.   Courage, brother,
Our fate is sealed. These tigers are athirst.
Return we to our people to proclaim
The gracious sentence of the noble court.
Let us go thank the Lord who made us those
To suffer, not to do, this deed. Be strong.

ACT V, SCENE 3

Within the Synagogue. Above in the gallery, women sumptuously attired; some with children by the hand or infants in their arms. Below the men and boys with silken scarfs about their shoulders.

    RABBI JACOB. The Lord is nigh unto the broken heart.*

---
* Service for Day of Atonement.

Out of the depths we cry to thee, oh God!
Show us the path of everlasting life;
For in thy presence is the plenitude
Of joy, and in thy right hand endless bliss.

 Enter SUSSKIND, REUBEN, *etc.*

 SEVERAL VOICES. Woe unto us who perish!

 A JEW.   Süsskind von Orb,
Thou hast brought down this doom. Would we had heard
The prophet's voice!

 SUSSKIND.   Brethren, my cup is full!
Oh let us die as warriors of the Lord.
The Lord is great in Zion. Let our death
Bring no reproach to Jacob, no rebuke
To Israel. Hark ye! let us crave one boon
At our assassin's hands; beseech them build
Within God's acre where our fathers sleep,
A dancing-floor to hide the fagots stacked.
Then let the minstrels strike the harp and lute,
And we will dance and sing above the pile,
Fearless of death, until the flames engulf,
Even as David danced before the Lord,
As Miriam danced and sang beside the sea.
Great is our Lord! His name is glorious
In Judah, and extolled in Israel!
In Salem is his tent, his dwelling place
In Zion; let us chant the praise of God!

 A JEW. Süsskind, thou speakest well! We will meet death
With dance and song. Embrace him as a bride.
So that the Lord receive us in His tent.

 SEVERAL VOICES. Amen! amen! amen! we dance to death!

 RABBI JACOB. Süsskind, go forth and beg this grace of them.
              [*Exit Süsskind.*]

Punish us not in wrath, chastise us not
In anger, oh our God! Our sins o'erwhelm
Our smitten heads, they are a grievous load;
We look on our iniquities, we tremble,
Knowing our trespasses. Forsake us not.
Be thou not far from us. Haste to our aid,
Oh God, who art our Saviour and our Rock!

Re-enter Süsskind.

SUSSKIND. Brethren, our prayer, being the last, is granted.
The hour approaches. Let our thoughts ascend
From mortal anguish to the ecstasy
Of martyrdom, the blessed death of those
Who perish in the Lord. I see, I see
How Israel's ever-crescent glory makes
These flames that would eclipse it, dark as blots
Of candle-light against the blazing sun.
We die a thousand deaths,—drown, bleed, and burn;
Our ashes are dispersed unto the winds.
Yet the wild winds cherish the sacred seed,
The waters guard it in their crystal heart,
The fire refuseth to consume. It springs,
A tree immortal, shadowing many lands,
Unvisited, unnamed, undreamed as yet.
Rather a vine, full-flowered, golden-branched,
Ambrosial-fruited, creeping on the earth,
Trod by the passer's foot, yet chosen to deck
Tables of princes. Israel now has fallen
Into the depths, he shall be great in time.*
Even as we die in honor, from our death
Shall bloom a myriad heroic lives,
Brave through our bright example, virtuous
Lest our great memory fall in disrepute.
Is one among us brothers, would exchange
His doom against our tyrants,—lot for lot?
Let him go forth and live—he is no Jew.
Is one who would not die in Israel
Rather than live in Christ,—their Christ who smiles
On such a deed as this? Let him go forth—
He may die full of years upon his bed.
Ye who nurse rancor haply in your hearts,
Fear ye we perish unavenged? Not so!
To-day, no! nor to-morrow! but in God's time,
Our witnesses arise. Ours is the truth,

---

* The vine creeps on the earth, trodden by the passer's foot, but its fruit goes upon the table of princes. Israel now has fallen in the depths, but he shall be great in the fullness of time.—TALMUD.

Ours is the power, the gift of Heaven. We hold
His Law, His lamp, His covenant, His pledge.
Wherever in the ages shall arise
Jew-priest, Jew-poet, Jew-singer, or Jew-saint—
And everywhere I see them star the gloom—
In each of these the martyrs are avenged!

    RABBI JACOB. Bring from the Ark the bell-fringed, silken-
                                                    bound
Scrolls of the Law. Gather the silver vessels,
Dismantle the rich curtains of the doors,
Bring the Perpetual Lamp; all these shall burn,
For Israel's light is darkened, Israel's Law
Profaned by strangers. Thus the Lord hath said:*
"The weapon formed against thee shall not prosper,
The tongue that shall contend with thee in judgment,
Thou shalt condemn. This is the heritage
Of the Lord's servants and their righteousness.
For thou shalt come to peoples yet unborn,
Declaring that which He hath done. Amen!"

    [*The doors of the Synagogue are burst open with tumultu-
ous noise. Citizens and officers rush in.*]

    CITIZENS. Come forth! the sun sets! Come, the Council waits!
What! will ye teach your betters patience? Out!
The Governor is ready. Forth with you,
Curs! serpents! Judases! The bonfire burns!

                                                    [*Exeunt.*]

---

    * Conclusion of service for Day of Atonement.

Translations

DONNA CLARA*

By Heine

In the evening through her garden
Wanders the Alcalde's daughter;
Festal sounds of drum and trumpet
Ring out hither from the castle.

"I am weary of the dances,
Honeyed words of adulation
From the knights who still compare me
To the sun—with dainty phrases.

"Yes, of all things I am weary,
Since I first beheld by moonlight,
Him my cavalier, whose zither
Nightly draws me to my casement.

"As he stands, so slim and daring,
With his flaming eyes that sparkle
From his nobly-pallid features,
Truly he St. George resembles."

Thus went Donna Clara dreaming,
On the ground her eyes were fastened,
When she raised them, lo! before her
Stood the handsome, knightly stranger.

Pressing hands and whispering passion,
These twain wander in the moonlight.
Gently doth the breeze caress them,
The enchanted roses greet them.

---

* From *Poems and Ballads of Heinrich Heine* translated by Emma Lazarus (N. Y., 1881). "Donna Clara" was first published in *The Jewish Messenger*, February 18, 1876, together with two Imitations that follow up suggestions in Heine's own notes: "Don Pedrillo," in which this son of Donna Clara and the Jew expresses his hatred of Jews to the Rabbi that he does not know to be his father, and "Fra Pedro," in which the boy, now an abbot, persecutes the Jews.

The enchanted roses greet them,
And they glow like love's own heralds;
"Tell me, tell me, my beloved,
Wherefore, all at once thou blushest."

"Gnats were stinging me, my darling,
And I hate these gnats in summer,
E'en as though they were a rabble
Of vile Jews with long, hooked noses."

"Heed not gnats nor Jews, beloved,"
Spake the knight with fond endearments.
From the almond-tree dropped downward
Myriad snowy flakes of blossoms.

Myriad snowy flakes of blossoms
Shed around them fragrant odors.
"Tell me, tell me, my beloved,
Looks thy heart on me with favor?"

"Yes, I love thee, oh my darling,
And I swear it by our Saviour,
Whom the accursed Jews did murder
Long ago with wicked malice."

"Heed thou neither Jews nor Saviour,"
Spake the knight with fond endearments;
Far-off waved as in a vision
Gleaming lilies bathed in moonlight.

Gleaming lilies bathed in moonlight
Seemed to watch the stars above them.
"Tell me, tell me, my beloved,
Didst thou not erewhile swear falsely?"

"Naught is false in me, my darling,
E'en as in my bosom floweth
Not a drop of blood that's Moorish,
Neither of foul Jewish current."

"Heed not Moors nor Jews, beloved,"
Spake the knight with fond endearments.
Then towards a grove of myrtles
Leads he the Alcalde's daughter.

And with love's slight, subtle meshes,
He hath trapped her and entangled;
Brief their words, but long their kisses,
For their hearts are overflowing.

What a melting bridal carol,
Sings the nightingale, the pure one!
How the fire-flies in the grasses
Trip their sparkling, torch-light dances!

In the grove the silence deepens;
Naught is heard save furtive rustling
Of the swaying myrtle branches,
And the breathing of the flowers.

But the sound of drum and trumpet
Burst forth sudden from the castle.
Rudely they awaken Clara,
Pillowed on her lover's bosom.

"Hark, they summon me, my darling.
But before I go, oh tell me,
Tell me what thy precious name is,
Which so closely thou hast hidden."

And the knight, with gentle laughter,
Kissed the fingers of his donna,
Kissed her lips and kissed her forehead,
And at last these words he uttered:

"I, Señora, your beloved,
Am the son of the respected,
Worthy, erudite Grand Rabbi,
Israel of Saragossa!"

TRANSLATIONS FROM THE HEBREW POETS OF MEDIAEVAL SPAIN

SOLOMON BEN JUDAH GABIROL
(Died between 1070-80)

NIGHT-THOUGHTS

Will night already spread her wings and weave
Her dusky robe about the day's bright form,
Boldly the sun's fair countenance displacing,
And swathe it with her shadow in broad day?
So a green wreath of mist enrings the moon,
Till envious clouds do quite encompass her.
No wind! and yet the slender stem is stirred,
With faint, slight motion as from inward tremor.
Mine eyes are full of grief—who sees me, asks,
"Oh, wherefore dost thou cling unto the ground?"
My friends discourse with sweet and soothing words;
They are all vain, they glide above my head.
I fain would check my tears; would fain enlarge
Unto infinity, my heart—in vain!
Grief presses hard my breast, therefore my tears
Have scarcely dried, ere they again spring forth.
For these are streams no furnace heat may quench,
Nebuchadnezzar's flames may dry them not.
What is the pleasure of the day for me,
If, in its crucible, I must renew
Incessantly the pangs of purifying?
Up, challenge, wrestle, and o'ercome! Be strong!
The late grapes cover all the vine with fruit.
I am not glad, though even the lion's pride
Content itself upon the field's poor grass.
My spirit sinks beneath the tide, soars not
With fluttering seamews on the moist, soft strand.
I follow Fortune not, where'er she lead.
Lord o'er myself, I banish her, compel,
And though her clouds should rain no blessed dew,
Though she withhold the crown, the heart's desire,

Though all deceive, though honey change to gall,
Still am I lord, and will in freedom strive.

A DEGENERATE AGE

Where is the man who has been tried and found strong
    and sound?
Where is the friend of reason and of knowledge?
I see only sceptics and weaklings.
I see only prisoners in the durance of the senses.
And every fool and every spendthrift
Thinks himself as great a master as Aristotle.
Think'st thou that they have written poems?
Call'st thou that a Song?
I call it the cackling of ravens.
The zeal of the prophet must free poesy
From the embrace of wanton youths.
My song I have inscribed on the forehead of Time,
They know and hate it—for it is lofty.

•   •   •

ABDUL HASSAN JUDAH BEN HA-LEVI

(Born between 1080-90)

LOVE-SONG

"See'st thou o'er my shoulders falling,
    Snake-like ringlets waving free?
Have no fear, for they are twisted
    To allure thee unto me."
Thus she spake, the gentle dove,
    Listen to thy plighted love:—
"Ah, how long I wait, until
    Sweetheart cometh back (she said)
Laying his caressing hand
    Underneath my burning head."

Prose

WAS THE EARL OF BEACONSFIELD A
REPRESENTATIVE JEW?*

. . . In order that a single man shall represent a people, it is certainly unnecessary that he shall embrace, in the most perfect degree, the whole gamut of qualities ever possessed by the united members of his race. . . .

Disraeli possessed in an eminent degree the capacity which seems to us the most characteristic feature of the Jew, whether considered as a race or an individual, and one which has been developed to perfection by ages of persecution. We refer to the faculty which enables this people, not only to perceive and make the most of every advantage of their situation and temperament, but also, with marvelous adroitness, to transform their very disabilities into new instruments of power. To-day, in Europe, their commercial prosperity is such as to arouse the jealousy and enmity of nations supposed to be the most enlightened, and yet this excessive accumulation of wealth is only the natural result of the stupid, not to say cruel, policy of those very nations in confining them for years to the practice of usury. Ostracized from the society of Christians, even when not made the victims of actual barbarity, refused a voice in the administration of public affairs, denied the honor of military service, excommunicated at the same time from legal protection and from Christian charity, it behooved them to organize all the more stringently their own little communities, to perfect their system of private beneficence, to administer their own affairs with scrupulous exactness, to practice the arts of peace, and to keep their eyes and wits ever open to the chance of gaining an inch of ground from the common enemy. . . .

. . . He belonged, by birth, to the branch of modern Jews known as the Sephardim, concerning whom an English writer has remarked: "Of the two large bodies of European Jews, the Ashkenazim, from Germany and Poland, and the Sephar-

---

* From *The Century*, April 1882. Emma Lazarus here rejects a position put forward by Georg Brandes in his book on Benjamin Disraeli (1804-1881) first published in 1878. Disraeli, born a Jew but baptized at the age of nine, was elected to Parliament as a Tory in 1837; became Prime Minister in 1866 for several years and then again in 1874, resigning in April 1880 because of protest against his Empire policy in Turkey, Afghanistan, and South Africa. He helped pass the great Reform Bill of 1867, enfranchising great numbers of workers.

dim, of Spanish and Portuguese descent, it is well known that during the Middle Ages the latter were the more eminent in wealth, literature, and importance. The general histories of modern Jews have treated of them as one people *per se*, without adequate consideration of how differently must have been modified the Judaism of Granada in the twelfth century, or of Castile in the fourteenth century, from that of the same period amid the ferocity and unlettered ignorance of Muscovy and Poland." There can be no doubt that a spark of fiery Castilian pride was transmitted, unstifled by intervening ages of oppression, to the spirit of Benjamin Disraeli. He knew himself to be the descendant, not of pariahs and pawnbrokers, but of princes, prophets, statesmen, poets, and philosophers, and in his veins was kindled that enthusiasm of faith in the genius and high vocation of his own people which strikes outsiders as an anomaly in a member of an habitually despised race. Indeed, in reading the annals of the mediaeval Jews of Granada, we meet with more than one instance of a career ascending from the humble station of the Hebrew scribe or shop-keeper to the premiership of the kingdom, which seems almost the counterpart of that of Lord Beaconsfield, and which he, doubtless, treasured in his mind as an earnest of future possibilities, no less than a proof of historic superiority. . . .

And yet the fact remains that Disraeli was not a first-class man; his qualities were not those of the world's heroes; he possessed talent, rather than genius; he was a sagacious politician aiming at self-aggrandizement, not a wise statesman building his monument in enduring acts of public service; and the study of his career is calculated to dazzle, to entertain, even to amuse, rather than to elevate, to stimulate, or to ennoble. But do all these derogatory facts preclude him from being considered a representative Jew? On the contrary, we think they tend to confirm his title. First-class men in all races are sufficiently rare, and they have not been absent from the annals of Judaism: Moses, Jesus, St. Paul, the prophets, Spinoza, bear glorious testimony to their existence. But centuries of persecution and the enforced narrowness of their sphere of action have, nevertheless, developed among the Jews a typical national character other than that of the above-named scions of the race. Adroitness, dexterity, tact, industry, perseverance, ambition, brilliancy, and imagination—these may be enumerated as their distinguishing qualities. Where shall we look for the great modern Jews? At the head of the revolutions, the politics, the finance, the journalism of Europe, or among actors, musical *virtuosi* and composers, wherever they can find a field for their practical ability, their long-starved appetite for power, their love of liberty, and their manifold talents. They are on the surface in every city of Europe and America where they have gathered in any considerable numbers. But in proportion as we seek among the less brilliant avenues to renown, among the slowly rewarded workers and students, we shall find fewer and fewer representatives of the race. . . .

RUSSIAN CHRISTIANITY VERSUS
MODERN JUDAISM*

The spontaneous action of the prominent citizens of London and New York, without distinction of creed, in protest against the Russian atrocities committed upon the Jews, happily renders unnecessary any denunciation on the part of a Jewess. In the April number of *The Century* Mme. Ragozin set forth the "Russian side" of the question, which appears to her sufficient explanation of a state of affairs characterized by the London *Times* as "a scene of horrors that have hitherto only been perpetrated in medieval days during times of war." Murder, rape, arson, one hundred thousand families reduced to homeless beggary, and the destruction of eighty million dollars' worth of property—such, in fewest words, are the acts for which an excuse is sought. The perusal of a single book—the work of Mr. Jacob Brafmann, a Jewish apostate in the pay of the Russian Government—has forever demolished, in her mind, the fallacy that the Christians have been persecuting the Jews, and has established in its stead the conspicuous fact that the Jews have been always, and still are, persecuting the Christians, especially in Russia. This great truth—that a handful of wretched Jews are "undermining the well-being" of the largest empire of the globe— Mme. Ragozin is confident will commend itself to the acceptance of all unprejudiced minds.

Let us first disabuse our readers of the sophistical distinction made by Mme. Ragozin, in common with many other writers, between the "two kinds of Jews," and the idea that

* From *The Century*, May 1882 in reply to "Russian Jews and Gentiles, from a Russian Point of View,' by Madame [Z.] Ragozin.

"a vast dualism essentially characterizes this extraordinary race." Behind this subtle error lurk all the dangers that have threatened the existence of the people, for whatever calumnies be refuted by a Jewish spokesman, the answer is ever ready: "These charges do not apply to you, and such as you. But how can you be sure that such outrages are not committed by some barbarous sect of your tribe?" Now, we *can* be sure of the Jews—more so, perhaps, than of any other people in the world, their history being the oldest among civilized nations, their social and moral code having remained unaltered through all time, and the vicissitudes of their fate having exposed them to almost every test which can affect individual or national character. The dualism of the Jews is the dualism of humanity; they are made up of the good and the bad. May not Christendom be divided into those Christians who denounce such outrages as we are considering, and those who commit or apologize for them? Immortal genius and moral purity, as exemplified by Moses and Spinoza, constitute a minorty among the Jews, as they do among the Gentiles, but here ends the truth of the matter. Facts disprove even the plausible theory that, where Judeaphobia has longest prevailed, there has been a corresponding fundamental degeneracy in the race, for their suppleness and elasticity seem almost without bounds. From the identical conditions which Mme. Ragozin describes in Russia as fatal to the moral and intellectual development of the Jews (the internal restrictions of the *Kahal* and the cramping tyranny of external laws) sprang in Germany, as soon as a breathing-place was opened, the generation of Moses Mendelssohn and his gifted family, including Felix, Fanny Hensel, and Dorothea Schlegel, Heine the poet, Edward Gans, Ludwig Börne, Doctor Zunz, Rahel von Ense, Henrietta Herz, and others. And to-day, after little more than fifty years of Jewish enfranchisement, the German Christians are making a piteous outcry that the Jews are usurping the intellectual, political and financial control of the state. . . .

There is but one answer to the charges against the Jews, which Brafmann professes to base upon quotations from the Talmud: they are singly and collectively false. They have not even the doubtful merit of originality, being simply a revamping of the wearisome old perversions, garblings, distortions, mistranslations of the spirit and letter of the text, which have been fully refuted by documents familiar to the whole reading public. For the subtle meaning of the Talmud we need not go to a bribed renegade and thief, who had the documents "abstracted" for him ("convey the wise it call!"), *not without danger,* by a friend from the Jewish archives." Charges of a similar nature to Mr. Brafmann's, but incomparably worse, were satisfactorily refuted two hundred years ago by Manasseh ben-Israel, in his famous petition to Oliver Cromwell.*

If a Moslem were to print an expurgated copy of the Bible, citing all the barbarous passages and omitting all the humane and noble features, what would Islam think of the corner-stone of Christianity? Yet this is precisely what the Jew-haters have done with the Talmud. Modern philosophical criticism, no less than a study of Jewish history, and a dawning appreciation of the nobility of the Jewish type of character, have dispelled among all thinking and cultivated minds the web of calumny spun by bigotry and folly around these remarkable volumes. . . .

That the Jews should ever form a hostile "state within the state" is rendered impossible by a solemn Biblical injunction commanding fidelity to the ruling government: "And seek the welfare of the city whither I have banished you, and pray in its behalf unto the Lord, for in its welfare shall ye fare well." [Jeremiah, xxix, 7. (Literally translated)] There is no such thing, therefore, as an independent disloyal Jewish community, in Russia or out of Russia. . . .

It is false that the Jews are "kept aloof by their own rulers" from modern culture. Witness the disproportionate number of Jews and Jewesses thronging the universities, to which they have only recently been granted admission. More than fifty per cent of the students at Kiev University are said to be Jews. They are not allowed, except in specially privileged cases, to live in Kiev proper; they live outside, and walk in and out of the town morning and night. There is but one limit fixed to the tyranny of Russian laws against Jews, and that is the caprice of absolutism. Over and above the law is enthroned the Czar. Hence, although until the year 1861 the Jews were literally re-

---

* On October 25-31, 1655 Menasseh came from Holland to London on Cromwell's invitation to deliver to him a Petition urging admission of the Jews to England, from which they had been banned in 1290. Graetz says: "Cromwell's followers, and the Republicans in general, were for their admission; Royalists and Papists . . . were opposed . . ." (*History of the Jews,* V. 44). After much public debate, the Petition was not openly granted, but in 1657 Cromwell authorized the opening of a Sephardic burial ground in London, thereby covertly lifting the ban.

duced to the level of pariahs by the stereotyped phrase "to all people, with the exception of the Jews," which followed every clause of the Russian code, the Czar reserves the arbitrary right to confer whatever honor he please upon any individual Jew.

If Russian Jews be as Mme. Ragozin represents them, they are what Russian Christians have made them. Was it not Heine who said: "Every country has the Jews it deserves"? Mme. Ragozin says the Jews are hated not because of different race, religion, dress, peculiar customs, etc., but because of their "servility, their abjectness, their want of manliness, their failure to stand up for themselves and resent injuries." Any one who aims at being as strictly logical as Mme. Ragozin might know that it is in vain to expect the virtues of freemen from a community of slaves. Of this same people, a prominent American Christian clergyman (Rev. Dr. Howard Crosby) publicly declared a few weeks ago: "It is the glory of America that she finds among the Israelites the purest and strongest elements of republican liberty." The Hon. J. W. Foster, late United States Minister at St. Petersburg, writes: "I do not mean to convey the impression that the Jews of Russia are equal in intelligence and social standing with their co-religionists of the most enlightened countries of Europe and America. Far from it. But they are superior in education and thrift to the same class among whom they belong." The cry against the Jews, in most countries where they have protection from the law, is not that they are servile, but that they are arrogant. . . .

That the Jews are as a rule shrewd, astute, and sharp at a bargain no one will deny; that a rapacious envy of their gains is at the bottom of all the religious and political outbreaks against them, I am as firmly convinced as is Mme. Ragozin herself. But none the less is it a fact that this envy, ashamed to appear under its proper name, seeks to disguise itself under the mask of any and every other sentiment—patriotism, self-preservation, religious zeal, righteous indignation in a thousand forms. But is it not as puerile as it is monstrous to assert that the Christians, who outnumber the Jews by millions, who have the whole power of the law and the throne to back them, not to speak of the prejudice of the whole civilized world in their favor, can find no other weapons than tyranny, violence, and murder to preserve them against the Jew, who has nothing but his wits? When Peter the Great was petitioned to grant the right of settling in Russia to a colony of Jewish merchants, he replied, jestingly, "Why, they would starve to death among the Russians."

Concerning Russian business habits, Bielinski, one of the most distinguished of their contemporary authors, writes: "When I go shopping in the city, while my ears are deafened and my human dignity is insulted by the vulgar policy of our national business community, advertising its own wares and almost forcibly dragging purchasers into the shops, then do I realize that I have fallen among the greatest swindlers in the world! What is to be done? The Russian is born so! We condemn this Asiatic ostentation, this cringing politeness bordering on servility, this shameless boasting, and can only say, like the fish to the angling-line, it has always been thus in Russia." ([Bielinski's works, ii, 28.] "Down with the Jews!" say the Loyalists; "they are at the bottom of Nihilism!" "'Down with the Jews and all the property-holding classes!' yell the Nihilists. "When the pitcher falls upon the stone," says the Talmud, "woe unto the pitcher! When the stone falls upon the pitcher, woe unto the pitcher! Whatever befalls, woe unto the pitcher!" . . .

THE JEWISH PROBLEM*

The Jewish problem is as old as history, and assumes in each age a new form. The life or death of millions of human beings hangs upon its solution; its agitation revises the fiercest passions for good and for evil that inflame the human breast. From the era when the monotheistic, Semitic slaves of the Pharaohs made themselves hated and feared by their polytheistic masters, till to-day when the monstrous giants Labor and Capital are arming for a supreme conflict, the Jewish question has been inextricably bound up with the deepest and gravest questions that convulse society. Religious intolerance and race-antipathy are giving place to an equally bitter and dangerous social enmity. This scattered band of Israelites, always in the minority, always in the attitude of *protestants* against the dominant creed, against society as it is, seem fated to excite the antagonism of their fellow-countrymen. Intellectually endowed, as M. de Lavelaye has remarked, with "a high ideality and a keen sense of reality" they may be said broadly to represent Liberalism and Revolution in Germany and Russia, Conservatism and Capital in England and America. Liberty they must and will have, but when this is once obtained, their energy is transferred to the aim of fortifying and preserving it. . . .

---

* From *The Century*, February 1883.

The Jew was usually forced to wear a badge or a peculiar costume, and in some places, branded on the chin in order to make him a more conspicuous mark for Christian contempt and hatred. He was imprisoned in ghettos, where he forgot the use of his mother-tongue and exchanged it for a Hebrew jargon which serves 'as a theme of amusement to the Jew-haters of to-day and as a convincing proof that German Jews are no Germans. After being robbed of his lands, he was excluded from all trades and all manual occupation. One alone remained open to him—and this one was *forced upon him by law*—usury. The first Jew who lived by lending money on interest was the learned Rabbi Jacob Tam, of France, whom crusading hordes had plundered in 1146. He complained bitterly of the necessity that forced upon him such an occupation: "We have been left no other branch of industry to support life and to pay the onerous taxes imposed upon us by your landed seigneurs." Bernard de Clairvaux admonished his followers, during the second crusade, against persecuting the Jews, because, if the Jews were not there, he said, "Christian usurers would deal more hardly by the people than the Jews did." In 1430 the Florentines betook themselves to the Jews of their city, who accepted lower rates of interest, in order to escape the extortions of Christian usurers. Centuries before the reproach of usury was raised against the Jews, organized bands of Christian usurers, under the name of Lombards, Etruscans, Florentines, Cahorsins, Ultramontanes, marched through Europe under the protection and recommendation of the Roman Curia, in order to enrich it by means of fraudulent loans and usury.

Of course only the wealthier Jews could lend money; the mass of the people were sunk in the deepest misery and condemned to labors which the Christians shrank from with loathing, to labors that degrade men and stamp upon them the mark of the Helot, the slave. . . .

. . . Let us leave, however, these revolting pages for a brighter side of their history; and before narrating their tardy emancipation, within the present century, and its brilliant results, let us glance at the one sunny spot which shines forth amid the mediaeval darkness. While the rest of Europe was buried in superstition and barbarism, the dominion of the Moors exempted a large part of Spain from the influences of the Church. Here the intellectual and moral development of the Jews had free scope, and we find them consequently engaged in all branches of productive industry—silk-merchants, dyers of purple, glass-manufacturers, as well as superintendents of the noble colleges founded by the Saracens, scholars, doctors, poets, statesmen, and philosophers. . . .

For fully three centuries there remained in Europe no spot of refuge for the luckless race, until the French Revolution, breaking a million chains, brought with it also their emancipation. Wherever the French rule was established, the Jews were accorded full rights of citizenship, but almost a century was needed to complete their enfranchisement throughout the rest of Europe—nor is it today completed. . . .

Even in America, presumably the refuge of the oppressed, public opinion has not yet reached that point where it absolves the race from the sin of the individual. Every Jew, however honorable or enlightened, has the humiliating knowledge that his security and reputation are, in a certain sense, bound up with those of the meanest rascal who belongs to his tribe, and who has it in his power to jeopardize the social status of his whole nation. It has been well said that the Jew must be of gold in order to pass for silver. Since the establishment of the American Union, Jews have here enjoyed absolute civil and political freedom and equality, and until the past few years, a large and in some places almost entire immunity from social prejudice. Their toleration, it is now asserted, has failed to produce beneficial results; on the contrary they have degenerated, rather than improved, under these favorable conditions. While I admit the fact that America has no such brilliant list of Semitic names as the Europe of today can show, I find nothing to support the theory of degeneracy of the race. Being subjected to the same influences as are the Christians who surround them, they simply evince the same proclivities. In this commercial country and commercial age they have been known chiefly as thriving merchants, tradesmen, and bankers who have enjoyed, as a rule, a high degree of credit and respect. If they have not surpassed, neither have they fallen behind, their competitors of other sects. . . . They have shared all national burdens and sorrows, fighting the battles of the Revolution and of the Union, grudging neither life nor money to the fortunes of the Republic. They are the prominent patrons of all musical enterprise—the only general division of art which has attained nearly as advanced a state of cultivation here as in Europe. The leader of free religious thought, and an indefatigable promoter of the better education of the poor in New York is a Jew—Felix Adler.* The race is represented in every liberal profession, in the army, the navy, and the house of Congress.

And yet here, too, the everlasting prejudice is cropping out in various shapes. Within recent years, Jews have been "boy-cotted" at not a few places of public resort; in our schools and colleges, even in our scientific universities, Jewish scholars are frequently subjected to annoyance on account of their race. The word "Jew" is in constant use, even among so-called refined Christians, as a term of opprobrium, and is employed as a verb, to denote the meanest tricks. In other words, all the magnanimity, patience, charity, and humanity, which the Jews have manifested in return for centuries of persecution, have been thus far inadequate to eradicate the profound antipathy engendered by fanaticism and ready to break out in one or another shape at any moment of popular excitement.

II.

. . . The insatiable thirst of the Jews is not for money, as calumniously asserted, but for knowledge. In those districts of Poland and Russia where they are refused admittance to the schools, they have had books of natural science and Darwinian treatises translated into Hebrew in order to follow the in-tellectual movement of the age. . . . The first use they make of their freedom invariably is to embrace all methods of higher instruction, and to strive toward a more complete intellectual development. It is assumed by Christian historians that the Jews, with their inflexible adherence to the Mosaic Code, are, as a people, a curious relic of remote antiquity, a social anachronism, so to speak, petrified in the midst of advancing civilization. This assumption is without foundation; the Jews are, on the contrary, most frequently the pioneers of progress. The simplicity of their creed enables them more readily and naturally to throw off the shackles of superstition and to enlarge the boundaries of free speculation than any other sect. Con-sidering their religion from the highest standpoint, their creed today is at one with the latest doctrines of science, proclaiming the unity of the Creative force. No angels, saints, or mediators have any place in this sublime conception, arrived at intuitively in a pre-historic age by the genius of the race, and confirmed by that modern scientific research which has revolutionized

---
* An American ethical reformer, 1851-1933.

77

the thought of the world. The modern theory of socialism and humanitarianism, erroneously traced to the New Testament, has its root in the Mosaic Code. The Christian doctrine is the doctrine of consolation; the kingdom of heaven is held out as a glittering dream to suffering humanity. Poverty exalted into a mission, the vocation of the mystic, the spiritualist, the idealist, enjoined equally upon all, a vision and an ecstasy offered to the hungry and the needy; what provision is here made for the world as it is? On the other hand, the very latest reforms urged by political economists, in view of the misery of the lower classes, are established by the Mosaic Code, which formulated the principle of the rights of labor, denying the right of private property in land, asserting that the corners of the field, the gleanings of the harvest belonged in *justice*, not in *charity*, to the poor and the stranger; and that man owed a duty, not only to all humanity, but even to the beast of the field, and "the ox that treads the corn." In accordance with these principles we find the fathers of modern socialism to be three Jews—Ferdinand Lassalle, Karl Marx, and Johann Jacoby.*

The melancholy and disgraceful fact being established that, in these closing decades of the nineteenth century, the long-suffering Jew is still universally exposed to injustice, proportioned to the barbarity of the nation that surrounds him, from the indescribable atrocities of Russian mobs, through every degree of refined insult to petty mortification, the inevitable result has been to arouse most thinking Jews to the necessity of a vigorous and concerted action of defense. They have long enough practiced to no purpose the doctrine which Christendom has been content to preach, and which was inculcated by one of their own race—when the right cheek was smitten to turn also the left. They have proved themselves willing and able to assimilate with whatever people and to endure every climatic influence. But blind intolerance and ignorance are now forcibly driving them into that position which they

---

* Lassalle (1825-1864); Karl Marx (1818-1883), founder of scientific socialism; Jacoby (1805-1877), Reichstag deputy from Berlin in 1870, author of a widely translated speech, "The Social Question." Marx fought Lassalle for betraying the people to Bismarck but respected Jacoby as a consistent democrat. On Nov. 19, 1870 Jacoby addressed a mass meeting at Cooper Union in New York to protest the continuation of the Franco-Prussian War. *The Workingman's Advocate* (Chicago), Dec. 3, 1870, states: "An enthusiastic demonstration of applause was given for Jacoby, the great German leader of the political-socialists movement in Germany . . ."

have so long hesitated to assume. *They must establish an independent nationality.* . . .

AN EPISTLE TO THE HEBREWS
Introductory*

It is a singular fact that the contemporary student of Jewish life and character derives chiefly from Christian sources, a faith in the regenerating powers of Judaism. The Jews themselves, especially those of America, seem rarely imbued with that vivid sense of the possibilities and responsibilities of their race, which might result in such national action as to justify the expectations (and in some cases the ignoble fears) of their Gentile critics. When one turns glowing with enthusiasm from the pages of George Eliot, of Gabriel Charmes, of Ernest Havet, of Lawrence Oliphant,** to the actual Jewish community amidst which we live, one is half tempted to believe that it is necessary to be born outside of Judaism in order to appreciate the full beauty and grandeur of her past, the glory and infinite expansiveness of her future. The unworthy desire on the part of many Jews to conceal their lineage, evinced in the constant transmutation of family-names, and in the contemptible aversion and hostility manifested between Jews of varying descent, painfully prove the absence of both the spirit and the training essential to a higher national existence. Fancy a self-respecting American, Englishman, Frenchman, etc., endeavoring to impose upon his neighbors the idea that he belongs to a race other than his own! Yet nothing is more common (and we may add, more futile) among the Jews. As long as every man respects the virtues and achievements of his ancestors, he is proud to claim his rightful lineage. Only when a deep and abiding sense of national humiliation has taken root, is it possible for men of ordinary honesty and intelligence to repudiate or shrink from acknowledgement of their descent. Nor have we in America the excuse for such national weakness as has been elsewhere

---

* From *The American Hebrew*, November 3, 1882 to February 23, 1883.
** Gabriel Charmes (1850-1886), democrat and friend of Heine, author of books on Egypt, Turkey, and Naval Reform; Ernest Havet (1813-1889), author of *Le Christianisme et ses origines* (1871-1884), Laurence Oliphant (1829-1888) in *Land of Gilead*, 1880, proposed a Jewish colony in Palestine; George Eliot (1819-1880) in *Daniel Deronda*, 1876, proposed the creation of a Jewish national land.

afforded up to our own day by the brutal Jew-baiting of European countries. A century of civil and religious equality has removed every extenuating circumstance that could be pleaded for it. . . . If I speak with occasional severity of the weakness or the degeneracy in certain points of my people, I premise that I do so with full appreciation of the heroic martyrdom of ages that has in great part engendered their national defects. Not for the sake of those who have mainly begotten in us the faults inseparable from long subjection to oppression and contempt, but for our own sakes, for the sake of the coming generation, I shall endeavor to impress upon my readers the urgent necessity for reform along the whole line of Jewish thought and Jewish life, and for a deepening and quickening of the sources of Jewish enthusiasm. . . .

II.

. . . It is very difficult for the modern student of history to insulate his mind so completely from the intellectual and moral conditions of the present as to adapt himself thoroughly to the limitations of an earlier age. And yet through only such a process is a true knowledge of the past accessible. Certain moral ideas are the birth of a very complex order of civilization and can only be developed in the slow progress of time. Such for instance is the idea of the sinfulness of slavery, which it would be as absurd to expect from the ancient Jew or Greek whose whole system of society was based upon the institution, as to look for a description of the telephone in Homer or the Bible.

Another such idea is the theory of Humanity as a grand whole towards whose common weal every individual must strive. This great idea dawned upon the mind of man about two centuries before the birth of Jesus, and was the natural result of the fusion of Greek and Hebrew thought. To the early Greek the world was divided into Greeks and Barbarians; the primitive Jew saw only "strangers," blasphemers and idolators in the nations that surrounded him. But when the Greeks were themselves swallowed up by the Barbarians, and the chief city of Hellenistic thought was no longer Athens but Rome, the Pagan poet formulated the immortal axiom: "I am a Man, and nothing that is human can be alien to me." Similarly when the Jews who had hitherto been acquainted only with intellectually inferior nations, suddenly found themselves face to face in Alexandria with the race that had invented philosophy and art, then they too awoke to the fact that good existed also outside of Judaism, and without abandoning their own intellectual stronghold, they proved as usual swift and prompt to assimilate all that was desirable in the surrounding civilization. The careful historical critic will find a gradual and orderly evolution of this idea of Humanity through the deepening and broadening charity of Deuteronomy and the Prophets, to the Rabbis of the Talmud including the immortal Hillel, and finally to the Alexandrian Jew [Philo, at time of Caligula] in whom the new doctrine of Universalism finds complete expression. From this time onward, the accusation of a narrow tribalism can never be made with justice against Judaism; it has imbibed and thoroughly assimilated the broad notion of a common humanity, by the light of which it interprets into a new significance the teachings of the older Prophets. . . .

To combine the conservation of one's own individuality with due respect for the rights of every other individuality, is the ideal condition of society, but it is a foolish perversion of this truth to deduce therefrom the obligation to renounce all individuality; and this remark is no less applicable to nations than to persons. Not by disclaiming our "full heritage," but by lifting up our own race to the standard of morality and instruction shall we at the same time promote the advancement and elevation of the Gentiles. Teaching by example, not by proselytism, has ever been the method of Israel. But he can fulfill his high vocation only on condition of maintaining himself at that level of moral and intellectual eminence where he becomes a beacon-light to others. To carry out this exalted conception we require a nation of priests, that is to say of priests in the best and original sense of the word—devoted servants of the holy spirit. But if our people persist in entrenching themselves behind a Chinese wall of petrified religious forms, the great modern stream of scientific philosophy will sweep past them, carrying Humanity to new heights, and will leave them far in the rear. The question is, where are we to look in America for the patriotic Jew whose intellect is sufficiently expanded to accept all the conclusions of science, and yet whose sense of the moral responsibilities and glories bequeathed to him by his ancestors is sufficietly vivid to kindle him into a missionary and a prophet? . . .

III.

Among the reproaches most frequently cast upon the Jews are their addiction to non-productive pursuits, their aversion to manual labor, their predilection for the fierce competitive strain of city barter and traffic. It is asserted that one rarely finds among the poorer classes skilled artisans and mechanics, trained servants or farm laborers; peddling, petty shopkeeping, pawn-brokerage, money-lending, hawking of old clothes or of old bottles, represent (it is claimed) their chief method of earning a livelihood. Among the wealthy or educated classes, stock jobbing, financial speculation, banking, trade, law and medicine constitute their principal occupations; in other words, rich and poor alike are disparagingly said to "live by their wits," rather than by the honest toil of industrious hands.

. . . As far as the above mentioned indictments are concerned, however, I wish to state distinctly at the outset *that they are partly true,* and that the observations of earnest Jewish workers in the fields of charity and social science give a certain amount of color to these imputations of our Christian censors. But while I have no hesitation in admitting the existence of the evil, I as emphatically deny and shall endeavor in the following paragraphs to disprove, that it is in any sense the outcome of racial characteristics or deficiencies, or that in our generation and country, the Jews are peculiarly and exclusively open to such reproaches. On the contrary, it may be rightfully claimed, that of all peoples, we are the only one in whom these particular national shortcomings are known to be the result of unjust legislation.

Antipathy to manual labor is one of the great social diseases of our age and country. . . .

. . . To all who can read the signs of the times, the evidences of a healthful reaction against this state of affairs are today everywhere conspicuous, in the springing up of industrial schools, the insistence of the public press and leaders of opinion upon the high value of technical training, and in the fascination exercised upon the young men of our large cities by the ranch-life of the West. All these encouraging signs, however, are only the beginning, and almost everything yet remains to be done, in order to imbue American minds with the true idea of the dignity of labor, and to train American hands to their worthiest vocation.

Like wheels within wheels, in the midst of this feverish, speculating, half-educated or falsely educated Plutocracy of America, we find a lesser community of Jews, to whom liberty and equality were even more novel possessions than to their Christian fellow-citizens, and yet who through perpetual bondage had never lost the love and the hope of freedom, or the ambition of material and intellectual distinction. What wonder if an overweening arrogance and ostentation were among the first outward tokens of emancipation from oppression and contempt? What wonder if in a people confined for centuries by foreign legislation to the lowest by-ways of petty traffic, we should find wits sharpened to super-subtlety by long practice in the arts of chaffering, bargaining and acquiring? What wonder if in the hearts of a people who for over a thousand years had found no other bulwark than wealth against the murderous hatred of Christendom, the desire of accumulating wealth had grown to be an hereditary instinct and one of the strongest passions.

And yet such were far from being the *normal* instincts and passions of the Jews. The Talmud says: "Get your living by skinning carcasses in the street if you cannot otherwise; and do not say I am a priest, I am a great man, this work would not befit my dignity." . . .

IV.

. . . Jewish historians delight to dwell upon the love of learning displayed by the Jews of the Talmud period and the early Christian centuries, in contrast with the mental darkness that prevailed around them. Jewish schools, and colleges such as the famous intellectual seats of Mehusa, Sura, Babylon, Nehardea and Pumbeditha* flourished in the midst of what has been aptly called a "mental wilderness." But cheering as this picture is, it has still another bright side which is not sufficiently taken into account. "These youths and men who attended the schools," says the eminent Talmudist, Dr. Jastrow, "were *farmers, mechanics, tradesmen,* none of them taking up learning as a means of support, or to speak Talmudically as a 'spade to dig with' . . . Jewish farmers devoting their leisure hours to study, Jewish youths and men twice a year, *when their agricultural pursuits would allow them a vacation,* streamed to the centers of learn-

---

* Famous academies flourished in Mehusa, Sura, Nehardea and Pumbeditha in Babylon from about the years 219 to 1000, when Babylonian Jewry was dominant in world Jewry.

ing." This is the feature of our past upon which it behooves us to insist at present. . . .

V.

. . . The second point on which I desire to insist is that our own people, in default of sufficient acquaintance with the wellsprings of our national life and literature, are apt to be misled by the random assertions of Gentile critics, and are often only too apt to acquiesce in their fallacious statements. "Tell a man he is brave, and you help him to become so," says Carlyle, and the converse proposition is equally true. Our adversaries are perpetually throwing dust in our eyes with accusations of materialism and tribalism, and we in our pitiable endeavor to conform to the required standard, plead guilty and fall into the trap they set. That our national temper and character have suffered grievous injury during our thousand-year-long struggle for existence is undeniable, but the injury has been precisely of an opposite nature to that which the world would have us believe. It has been a physical and material loss, as well as a loss of that homogeneity and united national sentiment which it is our first duty to revive in order to concentrate our efforts towards regeneration and rehabilitation. *"Tribal!"* This perpetual taunt rings so persistently in our ears that most Jews themselves are willing to admit its justice, in face of the fact that our "tribal God" has become the God of two-thirds of the inhabited globe, the God of Islam and of Christendom, and that as a people we have adapted ourselves to the varying customs and climates of every nation in the world. In defiance of the hostile construction that may be put upon my words, I do not hesitate to say that our national defect is that we are not "tribal" enough; we have not sufficient solidarity to perceive that when the life and property of a Jew in the uttermost provinces of the Caucasus are attacked, the dignity of a Jew in free America is humiliated. We who are prosperous and independent have not sufficient homogeneity to champion on the ground of a common creed, common stock, a common history, a common heritage of misfortune, the rights of the lowest and poorest Jew-peddler who flees, for life and liberty of thought, from Slavonic mobs. Until we are all free, we are none of us free. But lest we should justify the taunts of our opponents, lest we should become "tribal" and narrow and Judaic rather than humane and cosmopolitan like the anti-Semites of Germany and the Jew-baiters of Russia, we ignore and repudiate our unhappy brethren as having no part or share in their misfortunes—until the cup of anguish is held also to our own lips.

What we need today second only to the necessity of closer union and warmer patriotism, is the building up of our national, physical force. If the new Ezra arose to lead our people to a secure house of refuge, whence would he recruit the farmers, masons, carpenters, artisans, competent to perform the arduous practical pioneer-work of founding a new nation? We read of the Jews who attempted to rebuild the Temple using the trowel with one hand, while with the other they warded off the blows of the molesting enemy. Where are the warrior-mechanics of today equal to either feat? Although our stock is naturally so vigorous that in Europe the Jews remain after incalculable suffering and privation the healthiest of races, yet close confinement and sedentary occupations have un-deniably stunted and debilitated us in comparison with our normal physical status. For nearly nineteen hundred years we have been living on an Idea; our spirit has been abundantly fed, but our body has been starved, and has become emaciated past recognition, bearing no likeness to its former self. . . .

VI.

. . . "It is always the impossible which happens," said a witty Frenchman, and the axiom is applicable in a peculiar sense to the Jewish people. "A Jew may be a prophet, but cannot be a philosopher" the world once fancied, and the Jews produced a Philo, a Maimonides, a Spinoza. After we had been for centuries excluded from political life, we were told that a Jew could not be a statesman. But the external barriers were removed and within a single generation behold a Beaconsfield, a Lasker, a Gambetta.* . . . And now, as if the greater did not include the less, we hear on all sides the cry, "a Jew cannot be an agriculturist." Read the Reports of the colonies of refugees at Cotopaxi, Colorado, and Vineland, New Jersey, and you have facts and figures as a "victorious declaration of the truth that the Hebrew can be a farmer and is a farmer." The *Jewish Chronicle* tells us that "at Biella (Piedmont) there has lately been held an Industrial, and at

---

* Leon Gambetta (1838-1882), French Radical deputy and premier; Eduard Lasker (1829-1884), German publicist and Reichstag deputy, leader of the national Liberal party who helped achieve the unification of Germany.

Turin an Agricultural Exhibition. In both places Jews gained prizes."

In other words, a race whose spiritual and intellectual influence upon the world has been universally accounted second to none, and whose physical constitution has adapted itself to the vicissitudes of every climate, *can be whatever they will be.* Yes, we need only "help to will our own better future," and that future shall accomplish itself as by miracle. But as we are at present situated, whatever faculty we acquire only redounds to our ultimate disadvantage, and I know a warm Jewish patriot who grieves whenever he hears of a mark of distinction won by a Jew. For as soon as we adopt a new method of earning an honest livelihood, such skill as we happen to develop at it only brings down upon us from our unsuccessful competitors of other races the old charges of monopolizing and of mysterious tribal collusion. . . .

VII.

. . . For the most ardent supporter of the scheme does not urge the advisability of an emigration *en masse* of the whole Jewish people to any particular spot. There is not the slightest necessity for an American Jew, the free citizen of a republic, to rest his hopes upon the foundation of any other nationality soever, or to decide whether he individually would or would not be in favor of residing in Palestine. All that would be claimed from him would be a patriotic and unselfish interest in the sufferings of his oppressed brethren of less fortunate countries, sufficient to make him promote by every means in his power the establishment of a secure asylum. From those emancipated countries of Europe and America, where the Jew shares all the civil and religious privileges of his compatriots, only a small band of Israelites would be required to sacrifice themselves in order to serve as leaders and counselors. . . .

VIII.

. . . The fact that the Jews of America are civilly and religiously emancipated, should be, I take it, our strongest impelling motive for working towards the emancipation of our oppressed brethern. No other Jews in the world can bring to bear upon the enterprise such absolute disinterestedness of aim, such long and intimate familiarity with the blessings and delights of liberty. We must help our less fortunate brethren, not with the condescending patronage of the prosperous, who in self-defense undertake to conceal the social sores of the community by providing a remote hiding place for the outcast and the beggar, but with the keen, human sympathy of men and women who endeavor to defend men and women against outrage and oppression, of Jews who feel the sting of every wound and insult inflicted upon their bloodkindred. For ourselves, personally, we have nothing to ask or desire; neither our national nor our domestic happiness is bound up with the existence of any other Government in the world, than that of the United States. But by virtue of our racial and religious connection with these hapless victims of anti-Jewish cruelty, we feel that it devolves upon us to exert our utmost strength towards securing for them permanent protection.

It has become evident to a large majority of Jews that such permanent protection can never be afforded while masses of our people are concentrated in certain districts of Europe amidst hostile, or at least unfriendly, nations: where their free intellectual development is checked by legislative and social disabilities, and where at any moment an outbreak of popular fanaticism or the contagion of illiberal opinions may imperil their very existence. . . .

XI.

. . . However degrading or servile might be their avocations during the secular week, the first star of the Sabbath eve restored to them their human dignity, when they met in the Synagogue or around the family board, however humble, to sing, in the midst of bondage and oppression, those Psalms which have been for all ages, the battle cry of freedom, and to cherish the memory of days when they were a nation of princes and priests. The Sabbath was distinguished from the weekday by holiday apparel, by convivial gatherings, by music and gayety; the only limit to these was the equal right of every individual to undisturbed rest from labor. Whoever pauses to consider how large a part of the pleasures of the rich, depends upon the ceaseless toil of the poor, will see how great a proportion of daily amusement and luxury is cut off by this humane injunction. But such a restriction in modes of enjoyment, has nothing in common with the gloomy horrors of the Calvinistic Sunday, or the asceticism, the wearisome solemnity and repeated devotional exercises of the Puritans. Ours is the joyous spirit of the Roman Catholic Sabbath, with the simple difference that the humanity of the Jew never loses sight of the fact that in order to keep restaurants, theaters, concert and dancing-halls open on the day of rest, as in the gay Catholic towns of continental Europe, thousands of men and women are deprived of one of the greatest privileges ever accorded by legislation to the poor. Amid the actual conditions of our complex civilization, it would be neither desirable nor possible to revive in full force the Jewish Sabbath which was adapted to the needs of a comparatively simple agricultural society. But if there be any question of such a revival, let us at least understand what the Jewish Sabbath is, and not confound it with the stern and unpoetical Sunday of the New England Puritans, or with the ludicrous injunctions of the New York Sunday Penal Code. . . .

XIII.

. . . It will be a lasting blot upon American Judaism—nay, upon *prosperous* Judaism of whatever nationality—if we do not come forward now with encouragement for the disheartened and help for the helpless, or if we neglect this opportunity to dignify our race and our name by vigorous, united and disinterested action. To fail in such an attempt is no disgrace— the disgrace is in not undertaking it. Our own position of security places any efforts we make in this direction beyond the imputation of personal or unworthy motives. Our comparative remoteness from the scene of agitation enables us to judge oppressor and oppressed almost with the calmness of posterity. Our national American unconcern in the complicated entanglements of European politics, gives us a peculiar clearness of vision and coolness of head wherewith to measure the chances and advantages of international alliances. We possess the double cosmopolitanism of the American and the Jew. We see the leashed and greedy hounds of European power straining at their checks, ready to pounce upon the tempting morsel of Egyptian supremacy, or struggling to be freed for the chase and to be "in at the death" of the Ottoman Empire. We have only to watch and to wait, and to put ourselves in readiness for action upon an emergency. "The gods themselves," says a Chinese proverb, "cannot help him who loses opportunities." . . .

XV.

. . . The irresistible tendency of intelligent Judaism during the past century, has been towards leveling the barriers established in ages of persecution that separated us as a people from surrounding nations. Today, wherever we are free, we are at home. We contributed our share towards building up the fortunes of this Republic; we served our part in the war that indissolubly cemented the Union; our right of occupancy is as old as that of our Christian neighbors; we are ready and glad to pay the full price demanded equally of Spaniard and Englishman, of Teuton and Celt, of Jew and Christian, for the privileges of American citizenship, viz: the forfeiture of all claim to an alien nationality. . . .

XVI. (*Conclusion*)

. . . All that I wish most earnestly to implore from Jews of every variety of political and religious belief, is that they lay aside personal and superficial considerations and approach this subject in the grave spirit which it imperatively demands, and with the cordial desire to ignore all non-essential differences and to meet upon those bases of agreement which must underlie all patriotic Jewish thought, and upon which some substantial project of reform or emancipation may be consentaneously founded. The Jew (I say it proudly rather than deprecatingly) is a born rebel. He is endowed with a shrewd, logical mind, in order that he may examine and protest; with a stout and fervent heart in order that the instinct of liberty may grow into a consuming passion, whereby, if need be, all other impelling motives shall be swallowed up. Such a one reluctantly submits to the restraint of discipline, even if it be imposed by the exigencies of his peculiar lot, in the interests of his own race.

. . . To unite in concerted action a people so jealous of their individual privileges, is a task of such difficulty as to be generally deemed impossible. The lesson of discipline and organization is the last one that the Jews will learn; but until they have mastered it, they cannot hope to secure by desultory, independent and often mutually conflicting efforts, equal conditions and human rights for their oppressed brethren.

A BIOGRAPHICAL SKETCH OF HEINE*

. . . As the medical profession was in those days the only one open to Jews in Germany, the boy Heine was destined for a commercial career; and in 1815 his father took him to Frankfort to establish him in a banking-house. But a brief trial proved that he was utterly unsuited to the situation, and after two months he was back again in Düsseldorf. Three years later he went to Hamburg, and made another attempt to adopt a mercantile pursuit under the auspices of his uncle, the wealthy banker Solomon Heine. The millionaire, however, was very soon convinced that the "fool of a boy" would never be fit for a counting-house, and declared himself willing to furnish his nephew with the means for a three years' course at the university, in order to obtain a doctor's degree and practice law in Hamburg. It was well-known that this would necessitate Harry's adoption of Christianity; but his proselytism did not strike those whom it most nearly concerned in the same way as it has impressed the world. So far from this being the case, he wrote in 1823 to his friend Moser: "Here the question of baptism enters; none of my family is opposed to it except myself; but this *myself* is of a peculiar nature. With my mode of thinking, you can imagine that the mere act of baptism is indifferent to me; that even symbolically I do not consider it of any importance, and that I shall only dedicate myself more entirely to upholding the rights of my unhappy brethren. But, nevertheless, I find it beneath my dignity and a taint upon my honor, to allow myself to be baptized in order to hold office in Prussia. I understand very well the Psalmist's words: 'Good God, give me my daily bread, that I may not blaspheme thy name!' "

The uncle's offer was accepted. In 1819 Harry Heine entered the university of Bonn. . . . After a few months at Bonn, he removed to the university of Göttingen, which he left in 1822 for Berlin. There is no other period in the poet's career on which it is so pleasant to linger as on the two years of his residence in the Prussian capital. . . .

Not only his social and intellectual faculties found abundant stimulus in this bracing atmosphere, but his moral convictions were directed and strengthened by the philosophy and

---

* From *Poems and Ballads of Heinrich Heine,* translated by Emma Lazarus (N. Y., 1881).

personal influence of Hegel, and his sympathies with his own race were aroused to enthusiastic activity by the intelligent Jews who were at that time laboring in Berlin for the advancement of their oppressed brethren. In 1819 had been formed the "Society for the Culture and Improvement of the Jews," which, though centered in Berlin, counted members all over Prussia, as well as in Vienna, Copenhagen, and New York. Heine joined it in 1822, and became one of its most influential members. In the educational establishment of the *Verein,* he gave for several months three hours of historical instruction a week. He frankly confessed that he, the "born enemy of all positive religions," was no enthusiast for the Hebrew faith, but he was none the less eager to proclaim himself an enthusiast for the rights of the Jews and their civil equality.

During his brief visit to Frankfort, he had had personal experience of the degrading conditions to which his people were subjected.

The contrast between his choice of residence for twenty-five years in Paris and the tenacity with which Goethe clung to his home, is not as strongly marked as the contrast between the relative positions in Frankfort of these two men. Goethe, the grandson of the honored chief-magistrate, surrounded in his cheerful burgher-life, as Carlyle says, by "kind plenty, secure affection, manifold excitement and instruction," might well cherish golden memories of his native city. For him, the gloomy *Judengasse,* which he occasionally passed, where "squalid, painful Hebrews were banished to scour old clothes," was but a dark spot that only heightened the prevailing brightness of the picture. But to this wretched by-way was relegated that other beauty-enamored, artist-soul, Heine, when he dared set foot in the imperial Free Town. Here must he be locked in like a wild beast, with his miserable brethren every Sunday afternoon. And if the restrictions were a little less barbarous in other parts of Germany, yet how shall we characterize a national policy which closed to such a man as Heine every career that could give free play to his genius, and offered him the choice between money changing and medicine?

It was not till he had exhausted every means of endeavoring to secure a remission of the humiliating decree that he consented to the public act of apostasy, and was baptized in the summer of 1825 in the Lutheran parsonage of Heiligenstadt with the name of Johann Christian Heinrich. During the period of his earnest labors for Judaism, he had buried himself with fervid zeal in the lore of his race, and had conceived the idea of a prose-legend, the *Rabbi of Bacharach*, illustrating the persecutions of his people during the middle ages. . . .

. . . But a note of such tremendous power as Heine had struck in this romance, required for its prolonged sustention a singleness of purpose and an exaltation of belief in its efficacy and truth, which he no longer possessed after his renunciation of Judaism. He was no longer at one with himself, for no sooner was the irrevocable step taken than it was bitterly repented, not as a recantation of his principles—for as such, no one who follows the development of his mind can regard it,—but as an unworthy concession to tyrannic injustice. How sensitive he remained in respect to the whole question is proved most conspicuously by his refraining on all occasions from signing his Christian name, Heinrich. Even his works he caused to appear under the name of H. Heine, and was once extremely angry with his publisher for allowing by mistake the full name to be printed. . . .

During the summer of 1830, while he was loitering at Helgoland, he was roused to feverish excitement by the news of the July Revolution. He inveighed against the nobility in a preface to a pamphlet, called *Kahldorf on the Nobility*, which largely increased the number of his powerful enemies. The literary censorship had long mutilated his prose writings, besides materially diminishing his legitimate income by prohibiting the sale of many of his works. He now began to fear that his personal liberty would be restricted as summarily as his literary activity; and in May, 1831, he took up his residence in Paris. He perfected himself in the French language, and by his brilliant essays on French art, German philosophy, and the Romantic School, soon acquired the reputation of one of the best prose writers of France, and the "wittiest Frenchman since Voltaire." He became deeply interested in the doctrine of St. Simonism, then at its culminating point in Paris. Its central idea of the rehabilitation of the flesh, and the sacredness of labor, found an enthusiastic champion in him who had so long denounced the impracticable spiritualism of Christianity. He, the logical, clear-headed sceptic in all matters pertaining to existing systems and creeds, seems possessed with the credulity of a child in regard to every scheme of human regeneration, or shall we call it the exaltation of the Jew, for whom the Messiah has not yet arrived, but is none the less confidently and hourly expected? . . .

THE POET HEINE*

. . . A fatal and irreconcilable dualism formed the basis of
Heine's nature, and was the secret cause not only of his profound unhappiness, but of his moral and intellectual incon-
sistencies. He was a Jew, with the mind and eyes of a Greek.
A beauty-loving, myth-creating pagan soul was imprisoned in
a Hebrew frame; or rather, it was twinned, like the unfortu-
nate Siamese, with another equally powerful soul,—proud, re-
bellious, oriental in its love of the vague, the mysterious, the
grotesque, and tragic with the two-thousand-year-old Passion
of the Hebrews. In Heine the Jew there is a depth of human
sympathy, a mystic warmth and glow of imagination, a pathos,
an enthusiasm, an indomitable resistance to every species of
bondage, totally at variance with the qualities of Heine the
Greek. On the other hand, the Greek Heine is a creature of
laughter and sunshine, possessing an intellectual clearness of
vision, a plastic grace, a pure and healthy love of art for art's
own sake, with which the somber Hebrew was in perpetual
conflict. What could be the result of imprisoning two such
antagonistic natures in a single body? What but the contra-
dictions, the struggles, the tears, the violences that actually
ensued? For Heine had preeminently the artist capacity of
playing the spectator to the workings of his own mind, and
his mordant sarcasm and merciless wit were but the expression
of his own sense of the internal incongruity. . . . Today his
muse is the beautiful Herodias, the dove-eyed Shulamite;
tomorrow it will be the Venus Anadyomene, the Genius of
blooming Hellas. He laments the ruin of Jerusalem with the
heart-stirring accents of the prophets, he glorifies Moses, "the
great emancipator, the valiant rabbi of liberty, the terrible
enemy of all servitude! What a glorious personage!" he ex-
claims. "How small Mount Sinai looks when Moses stands on
its summit!" He confesses that in his youth he had never done
justice to this great master, nor to the Hebrew people. . . .

There was one ideal object from which Heine's loyal devotion never swerved nor wavered through all the vagaries of
his eccentric career—and this object was Germany. Harshly as
he and all his race were treated by the fatherland, his senti-

---

* From *The Century*, December 1884, written on the occasion of the
publication, in a German magazine, of a fragment of the lost "Memoirs
of Heine," which Emma Lazarus calls "this duplicate autobiography."

ment for the German people, his affinity with the German genius, his affection for the language, the literature, the legends, the very soil of his native land continued in unbroken force through all his years of exile beneath the thin veneer of Gallicism and cosmopolitanism. . . .

But if he loved Germany, it was the ideal, the possible Germany of the future, not the actual servile and petty principalities that constituted the Prussia of his day. He was never tired of ridiculing the "thirty kings or more," who "snored under the shadow of St. Gothard." When he returned to France after his last visit to his old home, he replied manfully to the "lackeys to the Government" who had taunted him with his partiality for the French and his want of patriotism: "I will honor and revere your colors," said he, "when they deserve my respect, when they cease to be an empty or a wicked farce. Plant the red, black and golden flag on the heights of German thought, make it the standard of free humanity, and I will shed for it my heart's best blood. Be easy; I love the fatherland just as much as you do. For this very love's sake I have pined thirteen years of my life in exile, and for this very love's sake I return today into exile, perhaps forever. . . . Be calm; I will never surrender the Rhine to the French, for one simple reason, because the Rhine belongs to me, by inalienable birthright. I am the free Rhine's freer son; on its banks stood my cradle, and I am unable to understand how the Rhine can possibly belong to any one but its own children. . . . As for Alsace and Lorraine, they will be united with Germany, when we have completed that which the French have begun, *when we outstrip them in act as we have already done in thought*, . . . when we have reinstated in their dignity the poor disinherited people, despised genius and disgraced beauty, as our great masters have said and sung, and as we young ones will do." . . .

Compared with these ringing, burning words, how cold seems the detached cosmopolitanism of Goethe, the serene pagan, the courtier and companion of princes, who, from his lofty heights of indifference, accused Heine, the embittered enthusiast, of a "want of love." . . .

. . . But it was the graft of a foreign tree that gave him his rich and spicy aroma, his glowing color, his flavor of the Orient. His was a seed sprung from the golden branch that flourished in Hebrew-Spain between the years 1000 and 1200. Whoever looks into the poetry of the mediaeval Spanish Jews will see that Heine, the modern, cynical German-Parisian, owns

94

a place among these devout and ardent mystics who preceded him by fully eight centuries. . . .

. . . The day before I visited his tomb the barrier-wall between the Jewish and Christian portions of the cemetery of Montmarte had been demolished by order of the French Government. As I saw the rubbish and wreck left by the work of humane destruction, I could not but reflect with bitterness that the day had not yet dawned beyond the Rhine, when Germany, free from race-hatred and bigotry, is worthy and ready to receive her illustrious Semitic son.

A DAY IN SURREY WITH WILLIAM MORRIS*

. . . There is no branch of work performed in Mr. Morris's factory in which he himself is not skilled; he has rediscovered lost methods and carefully studied existing processes. Not only do his artisans share his profits, but at the same time they feel that he understands their difficulties and requirements, and that he can justly estimate and reward their performance. Thus an admirable relation is established between employer and employed, a sort of frank comradeship, marked by mutual respect and good-will. . . . That the workman shall take pleasure in his work, that decent conditions of light and breathing-space and cleanliness shall surround him, that he shall be made to feel himself not the brainless "hand," but the intelligent co-operator, the *friend* of the man who directs his labor, that his honest toil shall inevitably win fair and comfortable wages, whatever be the low-water record of the market-price of men, that illness or trouble befalling him during the term of his employment shall not mean dismissal and starvation,—these are some of the problems of which Mr. Morris's factory is a noble and successful solution. For himself, he eschews wealth and luxury, which are within easy reach of his versatile and brilliant talents, in order that for a few at least of his brother men he

---

* William Morris (1834-1896), poet and Marxian Socialist, author of *The Life and Death of Jason* (1867), *Sigurd the Volsung* (1876), *The Earthly Paradise* (1868-1870), *The Dream of John Ball* (1888), *News from Nowhere* (1891), *How I Became a Socialist*, and *Chants for Socialists* (1885). In 1883 he joined the first Socialist body in England, the Democratic Federation, later known as the Social Democratic Federation, and became a political organizer for the movement. The excerpts are from *The Century*, July 1886.

may rob toil of its drudgery, servitude of its sting, and poverty of its horrors. . . .

In making the personal acquaintance of one whose artistic work is familiar and admirable to us, the main interest must ever be to trace the subtle, elusive connection between the man and his creation. In the case of Mr. Morris, at first sight, nothing can be more contradictory than the "dreamer of dreams born out of his due time," and the practical business man and eager student of social questions who successfully directs the Surrey factory and the London shop. . . .

The passion for beauty, which unless balanced by a sound and earnest intelligence is apt to degenerate into sickly and selfish aestheticism, inflames him with the burning desire to bring all classes of humanity under its benign influence. That art, together with the leisure and capacity to enjoy it, should be monopolized by the few, seems to him as egregious a wrong as that men should go hungry and naked. With this plain clue to the poet's character, there is no longer any contradiction between the uncompromising socialist and the exquisite artist of *The Earthly Paradise*. If Mr. Morris's poetry have (as I think no one will dispute) that virginal quality of springtide freshness and directness which we generally miss in modern literature, and which belonged to Chaucer as to Homer, the cause may be found in his reproduction in methods and principles of life of certain conditions under which classic art was generated. He has chosen to be a man before being poet; he has rounded and developed all sides of a well-equipped and powerful individuality; he has plunged vehemently into the rushing stream of current action and thought, and has made himself at one with his struggling, panting, less vigorous fellow-swimmers. He has not only trained himself intellectually to embrace with wide culture the spirit of Greek mythology, the genius of Scandinavian as of Latin poetry, but he has cultivated muscle and heart as well as nerve and brain. The result upon his art has been indirect, but none the less positive. . . .

Mr. Morris's extreme socialistic convictions are the subject of so much criticism at home, that a few words concerning them may not be amiss here. Rather would he see the whole framework of society shattered than a continuance of the actual condition of the poor. "I do not want art for a few, any more than education for a few or freedom for a few. No, rather than that art should live this poor, thin life among a few exceptional men, despising those beneath them for an ignorance for which they themselves are responsible, for a brutality which they will not struggle with; rather than this, I would that the world should indeed *sweep away all art for a while.* . . . Rather than the wheat should rot in the miser's granary I would that the earth had it, that it might yet have a chance to quicken in the dark."

The above paragraph from a lecture delivered by Mr. Morris before the Trades' Guild of Learning, gives the key to his socialistic creed, which he now makes it the main business of his life to promulgate. In America the avenues to ease and competency are so broad and numerous, the need for higher culture, finer taste, more solidly constructed social bases is so much more conspicuous than the inequality of conditions, and the necessity to level and destroy, that the intelligent American is apt to shrink with aversion and mistrust from the communistic enthusiast. In England, however, the inequalities are necessarily more glaring, the pressure of that densely crowded population upon the means of subsistence is so strenuous and painful, that the humane on-looker, whatever be his own condition, is liable to be carried away by excess of sympathy. One hears to-day of individual Englishmen of every rank flinging themselves with reckless heroism into the breach, sacrificing all thought of personal interest in the desperate endeavor to stem the huge flood of misery and pauperism. Among such men stands William Morris, and however wild and visionary his hopes and aspirations for the people may appear to outsiders, his magnanimity must command respect. No thwarted ambitions, no stunted capacities, no narrow, sordid aims have ranged him on the side of the disaffected, the agitator, the outcast. As poet, scholar, householder, and capitalist, he has everything to lose by the victory of that cause to which he has subordinated his whole life and genius. The fight is fierce and bitter; so thoroughly has it absorbed his energies, so filled and inspired and illumined is he with his aim, that it is only after leaving his presence we realize that it is to this man's strong and delicate genius we owe the enchanting visions of *The Earthly Paradise,* and Sigurd the Volsung, the story of Jason, and *The Aeneids of Virgil.*

M. RENAN AND THE JEWS*

. . . Like the breath of the mountain wind, Isaiah swept away, in these and many other familiar magnificent utterances, the whole rotten machinery of ritualism, feasts and fasts, sacrifices, oblations, and empty prayers. The prophets no longer call upon the children of Israel to go forth and make war upon nations whose lands they shall possess and inherit, but they are rallied to the cause of "bringing justice to the nations," of "establishing justice to the end of the earth." . . .

In the prophetic books are laid down, on broad bases, the foundations of a universal religion, a religion that preaches the purest, spiritual monotheism, the abolition of sacrifices and ritualism, the necessity of the moral law, the brotherhood of man, and the ultimate reign of peace and justice. Such, indeed, is the conclusion to which Christian scholars arrive. M. Renan continues: "The pure religion which we foresee, that will prove capable of rallying all humanity to its standard, will be the realization of the religion of Isaiah, *the ideal Jewish religion,* purged of the dross that may have been mixed with it. . . . Let us say boldly, Judaism which has done such service in the past will serve also in the future. It will serve the true cause, the cause of liberalism and of the modern spirit."

Such words as these send a thrill of exultation through the veins of every true Jew; not the unworthy pride of a flattered egotism, but the glorious sense of an inconceivably noble vocation. Nothing less than the universal welfare, bought at this price, could compensate the Hebrew race for having served through history as the type of suffering. Not for the mere survival of this little band of martyrs and victims was the miracle of their endurance prolonged; but because the seed of truth, which they alone cherished through fire and blood, had not yet borne its highest, sweetest and ripest fruit. "Christianity," says

---

* From *The American Hebrew,* October 24, 1884. This essay won first prize in a contest conducted by the Philadelphia Young Men's Hebrew Association. Emma Lazarus takes as her point of departure two lectures by Renan, one in January 1883, "Judaism as a Race and Religion," the other in May 1883, "Judaism and Christianity." Ernest Renan (1823-1892) became Professor of Hebrew, Chaldaic and Syrian Languages at the College de France in January 1862, and published his *Life of Jesus* in 1863 and his *History of the People of Israel,* 1887-1894. His liberal views made him a center of controversy and an object of attack by reaction.

M. Renan, "is Judaism adapted to Indo-European taste, Maho-metanism is Judaism adapted to Arabic taste." . . .

HENRY WADSWORTH LONGFELLOW[*]

. . . He belongs, intellectually and artistically to the genera-tion of Washington Irving, rather than to that of his actual contemporaries, Emerson or Walt Whitman; all his links are with the past; the legendary, the historic, enchanted him with an irresistible glamor; not only was he without the eyes of the seer, to penetrate the well of the future, but equally without the active energy or the passionate enthusiasm of an inspired cham-pion in the arena of the present. A pensive gentleness, a fluent grace, a tender sympathy with the weak, the suffering, the op-pressed, with loving women and with little children, and above all, an exquisite delicacy of taste, and an admirable skill of work-manship—these are the distinguishing characteristics of his poetry. He was too sincere to content himself with imported schemes, although he was not sufficienty endowed with original strength to found a new school. Hence, even when he chose an American subject, as in "Evangeline," "Miles Standish," or even "Hia-watha," his point of view and his method of treatment remained essentially European. . . . Here is no painful crudity of rough strength, no intellectual or moral audacity engendered by demo-cratic institutions, and by unprecedented vistas of a broadly de-veloping nationality. All is harmony, sweetness, and purity. Reversing Burns' process of setting new songs to old music, Long-fellow, as it were, takes a new tune and adapts it to well-re-membered words. One could almost guess from any volume of his poems, what great poet he was reading at the time, and by what foreign influence he was dominated. . . .

It is scarcely necessary to recall to Jewish hearers the well known lines, "In the Jewish Cemetery at Newport," wherein Longfellow's tender humanity finds sweet and pathetic expres-sion. These lines, in their almost colloquial simplicity, and their use of sacred, legendary or symbolic terms for purposes of homely illustration, are very characteristic of his method. . . .

Jewish readers will not be so willing to accept the concluding stanzas of the poems:

---

[*] From *The American Hebrew*, April 14, 1882; written for the Long-fellow Memorial Meeting of the Young Men's Hebrew Association, April 8, 1882, only two weeks after his death on March 24, 1882.

And thus forever with reverted look
   The mystic volume of the world they read,
Spelling it backward, like a Hebrew book,
   Till life became a legend of the Dead.

But ah! what once has been shall be no more!
   The groaning earth in travail and in pain
Brings forth its races, but does not restore,
   And the dead nations never rise again.

The rapidly increasing influence of the Jews in Europe, the present universal agitation of the Jewish question, hotly discussed in almost every pamphlet, periodical and newspaper of the day, the frightful wave of persecution directed against the race, sweeping over the whole civilized world and reaching its height in Russia, the furious zeal with which they are defended and attacked, the suffering, privation and martyrdom which our brethren still consent to undergo in the name of Judaism, prove them to be very warmly and thoroughly alive, and not at all in need of miraculous resuscitation to establish their nationality....

THE LAST NATIONAL REVOLT OF THE JEWS*

In the year 135 of the Christian Era, 3895 of the Jewish Calendar, occurred the final separation between the body and soul of Judaism, in other words, the definite extinction of Israel's national and political life and the beginning of its purely spiritual existence. The final death-struggle has a peculiar interest for American Jews, not merely because it was illustrated by deeds of heroic valor and endurance, but because it represents the very principle of revolt and independence upon which our present nation state is based. On the day that Bethar fell the Jewish Idea, the idea of protest, of revolution against moral tyranny, of inviolable freedom of thought and conscience, disenthralled itself from the limits of a narrow plot of soil, to be dispersed and disseminated for beneficent action over the entire globe. As the first destruction of Jerusalem had scattered the Jewish seed all over the Orient, so from the final war with Hadrian dates the dispersion of the Jews over the West. This "war of extermina-

---

* From *The American Hebrew*, November 14, 21, and 28, 1884. The paper was read before the Philadelphia Young Men's Hebrew Association on November 12, 1884.

tion," as the Talmud calls it, a war of despair, undertaken by the smallest of nations against the greatest, could necessarily have but one end. But the courage and skill with which it was conducted are proved by the fact that despite tremendous odds it was prolonged through three years, and that Rome, in order to extinguish it, was forced to summon from a distant province her most illustrious general and her bravest legions. Its captain perished, sword in hand, its chief councillor, the sage Akiba, was tortured to death by the conquerors, the lives of half a million Jews were sacrificed in its support, and yet, in accordance with the world's customary ingratitude towards the unsuccessful brave, a cloud of neglect and obloquy has, until a very recent date, enshrouded the figure of its leader, Bar-Kochba. . . .

When Hadrian ascended the imperial throne in 117, the active or sullen resistance of the Jewish people against the Roman yoke had already lasted nearly two centuries. . . . "That which increased the anger of the Roman people," says Tacitus, "was that the Jews alone refused to yield." . . . But neither argument nor force could prevail against these "irreconcilables"; always either actively militant, or else after sanguinary defeats secretly preparing new methods of resistance, the Jews may be said, single-handed, to have kept alive the flickering spark of liberty amidst the universal gloom of Roman servitude. . . .

This monarch, recognizing Judea as a dangerous centre of turbulent factions, resolved to annihilate its nationality and blot out the very name of Jerusalem. . . . From Egypt his commands were issued that the plough be passed over the ruined sites of the Temple, that the rite of circumcision be abolished, and that Jerusalem be rebuilt as a Pagan city. . . . These three fatal measures were the signal for revolt, the Sanhedrin was convoked with Akiba at its head, and a war for death or victory was unanimously resolved upon.

The rebellion seemed to break out over night: while, during Hadrian's visit, all Palestine had appeared tranquilly submissive, on the morrow of his departure two hundred thousand Jews sprang to arms. The movement, however, was less sudden than it appeared, otherwise, it would have lacked the organized force and solidity which it actually evinced in the three years' struggle. Placid as Judea had seemed in the eyes of her imperial guest, she was in reality in a state of violent inward ferment. . . . The Jewish artisans who were in the habit of supplying arms to the Roman soldiers, were found to have deliberately manufactured weak and worthless weapons. Judea was honeycombed with subterranean caves underneath its chalky hills, and in these the conspirators had met and not only perfected their deep and cautious plans, but had deposited their own skillfully wrought weapons of defense. The venerable Rabbi Akiba, the head of the community, had taken secret but active steps toward strengthening, extending and consolidating the general movement. He had traveled far and wide, instigating to revolt the Jews of Parthia, Asia Minor, Cappadocia, Phrygia and Galatia. When, therefore, the insurrection broke out, everything was in readiness—arms, methods of communication, soldiers and even a leader. This leader was Bar-Kochba,—"The Son of a Star," who seems to embody in one last supreme manifestation the martial spirit of his people. At his side the patriarchal figure of Akiba represents the intellectual and moral resistance to oppression, which still eminently distinguishes the Jews among all peoples of the earth. . . . The Jews of all the neighboring lands flocked to his standard; even their immemorial adversaries, the Samaritans, enrolled in his ranks, which were further swelled by troops of disaffected Pagans who made common cause with the Israelites in hope of shaking off the intolerable dominion of Rome. . . .

. . . Inch by inch the Latins regained the territory that Bar-Kochba had recovered from them in his brief campaign. Fifty-two distinct engagements had occurred, when the circle of Jewish possessions, gradually narrowing, had reduced itself to a single spot, and the whole Jewish army was beseiged in the town of Bethar. Within the walls, the Son of a Star, the last King of the Jews, directed and organized the defense, and punished with death whoever spoke of yielding, while the aged Akiba stimulated the beleaguered army with the example of his fortitude and patriotism, and presided over the Council of Ten who aided and advised the miltiary leaders. Thus all the forces that Judea held, of desperate courage, disciplined rebellion, religious zeal, unquenchable love of liberty, military genius and moral wisdom, were united for the final struggle and entrenched in Bethar.

. . . The siege lasted a year; when it became evident that the end was approaching, a very old man, Rabbi Eleazar Hamodai, proclaimed that the only hope left was in prayer, and day and night he fasted and watched upon his knees in a conspicuous position, praying for Bar-Kochba's success. . . .

. . . A general massacre of the inhabitants followed the entrance of the Roman troops, whose horses waded to the neck in blood. . . . Akiba and the nine rabbis who with him had formed

the council of defense were condemned to death by torture. . . .
Akiba was the last to suffer, being compelled to witness the agon-
ies of all his companions. He was burned at the stake, and his
flesh torn with iron instruments. . . .

. . . A dismembered nation, a territory laid waste and usurped
by the stranger, a prohibited religion, a Temple blotted from the
earth, a capital wiped out of existence in name and fact, and a
decimated tribe of exiles and slaves,—such were the immediate
results of the last fatal revolt of the Jews in 135. . . . But no!
through all history was to run the dark, rich stream of Jewish
life and thought, sometimes dwindling into a mere pulsing
thread, sometimes broadening into a powerful current, intersect-
ing or flowing parallel with all the great historic streams, never
losing its peculiar force and virtue. . . .

I have said that the last national struggle of the Jews had a
peculiar interest for American Israelites. In that little Judaic
tribe, wrestling for freedom with the invincible tyrant of the
world, I see the spiritual fathers of those who braved exile
and death for conscience's sake, to found upon the New England rocks, within the Pennsylvania woods over this immense
continent, the Republic of the West. I see in Bar-Kochba, the
ignored, despised, defeated Jewish soldier, the same passion
of patriotism which under more fortunate conditions, made illustrious a William of Orange, a Mazzini, a Garibaldi, a Kossuth,
a Washington. . . .*

EMMA LAZARUS TO HENRY GEORGE

[It has already been noted in the introduction that Emma Lazarus
was interested in the advanced thinking of her time. This hitherto
unpublished letter to Henry George (1839-1897), the economic
radical and reformer, is further evidence of her responsiveness to
progressive ideas. In 1879, George had published his masterpiece,
Progress and Poverty, vividly exposing the economic injustices of
our system and describing the mass misery that accompanied the
concentration of wealth. The book at once became a center of
controversy, and was attacked by those who feared the exposure of
social sores. Although its single-tax proposals were even then
impracticable and were based on the unsound theory that land was
the source of all value, the book stimulated reform movements in

---

* William of Orange was King of England when the Constitution of 1689
was adopted; Giuseppe Mazzini (1805-1872) and Giuseppe Garibaldi
(1807-1882) were patriots of the Italian democratic revolution. Lajos
Kossuth (1802-1894) was the leader of the Hungarian revolution of 1848.

which organized labor at the time took part. By 1881, when Emma Lazarus wrote this significant letter the work was in its fourth edition. Emma Lazarus had apparently made the acquaintance of Henry George some time after August, 1880 when he moved from California to New York.—M.U.S.]

New York
34 East 57th St.
October 17th, 1881.

My Dear Mr. George—

Pray accept my warmest thanks for your extremely kind note & for the eloquent pamphlet which I had already read & deeply appreciated, but which I need scarcely say will have a priceless additional value for me as coming from your own hands. I regretted more than I can say, the loss of your promised visit, & indeed, I curtailed my stay in the country in order not to miss the possible chance of seeing you—. To my great disappointment I saw by the papers that you had already sailed* on the day of my return. The receipt of your generous note was therefore a pleasure as unexpected as it was gratifying.

I wish I could convey to you an idea of the feelings aroused in me by your book. No thinking man or woman in these days can have remained altogether deaf to that mute "appeal which once heard can never be forgotten"; but the same appeal when interpreted by your burning eloquence, takes possession of one's mind & heart to such a degree as overpowers all other voices— Your work is not so much a book as an event—the life & thought of no one capable of understanding it can be quite the same after reading it,— & even in the small circle of my personal friends I have had abundant evidence of the manner in which it sets the minds of men on fire—"all men capable of feeling the inspiration of a great principle." And how should it be otherwise? For once prove the indisputable truth of your idea, & no person who prizes justice or common honesty can dine or sleep or read or work in peace until the monstrous wrong in which we are all accomplices be done away with— I congratulate you most heartily on the natural gifts with which you have been endowed for the noble cause you have espoused

---

* On October 15, 1881, Henry George had sailed for Ireland with his wife and two daughters, as correspondent for the *Irish World* in New York. His pamphlet, *The Irish Land Question*, had been published in New York and London the same year.

—Great as is the idea, it would certainly fail to kindle men's minds as it does now, if pleaded with less passionate eloquence, less authoritative knowledge.

I am glad to hear that your stay abroad is to be a short one, for I shall allow myself the pleasure of looking forward confidently to the hope of seeing you on your return.* We have many mutual friends besides Mr. Lindau,** all of whom have talked to me of you with the same enthusiasm— But I am proud to think that I need not rely upon any one else to bring us together. We have spoken with each other & know each other's voices, & at the end of six months or of six years, if I were still here, I should be no less sure of your sympathy & friendly remembrance. Meantime with earnest wishes for yourself & your cause, believe me

Gratefully & sincerely yours,

Emma Lazarus.

Henry George, Esquire.

---

* George returned to New York early in October, 1882, but it is not known whether Emma Lazarus met him then.
* * This was Leopold Lindau, a librarian.

APPENDIX

EMMA LAZARUS' INTEREST IN THE JEWS

It is pointed out by Henrietta Szold in *The Jewish Encyclopedia* that the Lazarus family, although "ostensibly Orthodox in belief," had not, by 1883, "participated in the activities of the Synagogue or of the Jewish community." And the Rev. Dr. Gustav Gottheil, in his eulogy at Temple Emanu-El after her death, records the following: "For some years before 1882, I had asked her aid in the work I had already at that time in hand, of issuing a hymn-book for Jewish worship. Her reply was, 'I will gladly assist you as far as I am able; but that will not be much. I shall always be loyal to my race, but I feel no religious fervor in my soul.'" When Dr. Gottheil's *Hymns and Anthems Adapted for Jewish Worship* appeared in 1887 there was an index to what Emma Lazarus meant by "as far as I am able." The volume contains her versification of Ecclesiastes, XII, and two of her translations from Moses Ben Ezra, together with much other work by Harriet Beecher Stowe, Whittier, Emerson, William Cullen Bryant, Longfellow, Robert Burns, and Harriet Martineau. Now unless one insists on identifying Jewish consciousness with "religious fervor" one could not support the interpretation of the complete suddenness of the change; it is noteworthy that Dr. Gottheil himself, deploring her indifference to religion, praises her loyalty to Jewry.

On the positive side, the following evidence exists. In her book, *Admetus* (1871), there is the poem written in 1867, "In the Jewish Synagogue at Newport." Those who consider this poem "detached," "impersonal," or lacking in "kinship with these dead Jews" might do well to compare the treatment of the theme with the poem in the same volume, "In a Swedish Graveyard." It is noteworthy that the poem was immediately reprinted in *The Jewish Messenger* of May 5, 1871, and again on March 29, 1872. And Henry Samuel Morais, in *Eminent Israelites of the Nineteenth Century,* published in 1880, *before* the developments that are held responsible for the too sudden change, wrote: "Her lines on the Jewish Synagogue at Newport are full of pathos anl religious sentiment." The poem is included within for the reader to make his own estimate. If one wants a clue to the difference between her consciousness of Judaism in 1867 and in 1882, one can examine in this connection her stricture on the last stanza of Longfellow's poem on the same theme (see pp. 99-100). In one she thinks only of the Jews of the past; in the later one, of the Jews of the vital present.

But even when the subject was not specifically Jewish, and most of her poems of that period were not, sometimes her phrasing will reveal her, as in the first two lines of "The Day of Dead Soldiers, May 30, 1869," written on the second Memorial Day:

Welcome, thou gray and fragrant *Sabbath-day,*
To deathless love and valor dedicate!

Then there is her *life-long* interest in Heine: her first translations of his poems appeared in 1867, her last article on him in December 1884, less than three years before her death. She was not only an excellent translator of this poet so difficult to translate well. Having translated "Donna Clara" (see p. 62), she was also stimulated to write two "Imitations," "Don Pedrillo" and "Fra Pedro," in which she fulfills what she declares to have been Heine's original intention. Yet the translations and the imitations together were first published in *The Jewish Messenger* for February 18, 1876. Can one read the poem, with its last lines orotund with the pride in Jewry, without realizing that Heine and Emma Lazarus were sharing a common triumph and a common knowledge of the nature of persecution?

It is also commonly assumed that her interest in the medieval Spanish Hebrew poets, and her translations of their poems, date from the period after 1881-1882. But here the record to the contrary is unmistakable: translations by Emma Lazarus of poems of Gabirol are published in *The Jewish Messenger* for January 17 and January 31, 1879, while translations from Judah Halevy appear in the same periodical in the issues of January 24, February 7, February 14, and February 21, 1879. These translations, it is specified, are from the versions in German made by Dr. Michael Sachs and Prof. Abraham Geiger, but they are the ones later included in the 1889 edition of *The Poems of Emma Lazarus.* While it is true that she did not begin to study the Hebrew language, under the guidance of Mr. Louis Schnabel and/or others, until the later period, her enthusiasm for a Gabirol and a Halevy, perhaps stimulated by Heine, is of much earlier date.

The final consideration in tracing the progress of Emma Lazarus' growing interest in Jewishness to the point where a definite qualitative change is noticeable is the date of *composition* of her impressive play, *The Dance to Death.* The family's biographical sketch, followed of course by most other writers, accepts as fact the theory that the work was written in 1882, as a reaction to the Russian pogroms. Contrary and apparently conclusive evidence is offered, however, by Mr. Philip Cowen, printer of *The American Hebrew* in Emma Lazarus' time. In *The American Hebrew* for July 5, 1929, in "Recollections of Emma Lazarus," he quotes a letter from Emma Lazarus herself, received by the editors of *The American Hebrew* on May 25, 1882, in which she wrote: *"A few years* ago I wrote a play founded on an incident of medieval persecution of the Jews in Germany, which I think it would be highly desirable to publish now, in order to arouse sympathy and to emphasize the cruelty of the injustice done to our unhappy people. I write to ask if The American Hebrew Publishing Company will undertake to print it in pamphlet form. . . ." (My emphasis.—M.U.S.)